The Merchant of Venice

A Romantic Comedy
by William Shakespeare

Editor: Edward Prendergast

FOLENS

Editor
Deirdre O'Neill

Design
Karen Hoey

Layout
Oisín Burke

ISBN 978-1-84741-193-8

Contents

Preface

The notes which accompany this edition of *The Merchant of Venice* are not intended as a substitute for reading and studying the play itself, nor do they dispense with the need for a teacher's guidance in that reading and study. Rather they provide lines of approach which are intended to stimulate interest and increase the student's own understanding, appreciation and enjoyment of the play. Used properly, they can act as a trigger to fruitful discussion as the student achieves his/her own individual view of *The Merchant of Venice*.

The Explanatory Notes alongside the text are designed to help towards an understanding of the more difficult words or phrases.

(a) A *summary* to help the student to understand what happens in each scene.

(b) *Scene Analysis* to suggest the significance of each scene in building up the play as a whole.

(c) *Character Analysis* to help the student to understand the people in the play and the reasons or motives for what they do or say.

Finally, the section on Further Study contains:

(a) A short essay examining the genre of the play.

(b) Suggested themes from the play.

(c) Context questions.

(d) Questions on individual scenes.

(e) Past examination questions.

(f) General questions on the play.

Part 1

INTRODUCTION

Shakespeare's Life and Work

William Shakespeare was born in April 1564 in Stratford-on-Avon. He was the third child of John Shakespeare, a prosperous merchant, and Mary Arden, the daughter of a substantial landowner, who were for a time reasonably wealthy and owned property in Stratford. In 1582, at the age of eighteen, William Shakespeare married Anne Hathaway who was eight years his senior. They had three children, Suzanna, Hamnet and Judith. Later, Shakespeare went to London where he joined the Lord Chamberlain's company of actors and made his name and his fortune as a writer of dramas. In a period of just over twenty years, he wrote thirty-seven plays, and a handful of long narrative poems together with the finest and most complete sonnet sequence in the English language. He retired to Stratford about 1611 where he had purchased 'New Place', one of the finest houses in the town. He died there on 23 April1616 and was buried at Stratford Parish Church.

Shakespeare's dramatic writings consist of comedies, histories and tragedies. He is best remembered for his great tragedies, *Hamlet, Othello, King Lear* and *Macbeth*, which were written between 1601 and 1607. Of his poetry, the sonnets, dealing with such themes as love, friendship and the ravages of time, are most memorable. His works, taken as a whole, exhibit a mastery of language, a range of emotion and an understanding of character which is unmatched in the English, or perhaps any, language.

The Merchant of Venice

The *Merchant of Venice* was written by William Shakespeare probably in 1596 and is one of his romantic comedies. The various stories of which the plot is made up were familiar to the people of Shakespeare's day. Among the sources he borrowed from most heavily was a collection of stories called *Il Percorone* by the Italian writer Ser Giovanni Fiorentino whose *Novelle* were bestsellers in Elizabethan England. Other elements came from the *Gesta Romanorum*, a collection of medieval tales from a Greek monk in Syria published in revised edition by Richard Robinson in 1595. He may also have had before him a play called *The Jew,* of which there are traces as early as 1579.

Whatever his sources, Shakespeare adapted them to suit his own purposes and what emerged is one of his most enduring masterpieces. Though it is more than four hundred years since it was written, *The Merchant of Venice* continues to be performed and to draw large audiences. It has something for everyone: love interest; interesting characters; comedy; elements of the tragic; music; poetry; a good story and a happy ending.

It is most famous perhaps for the character of Shylock – a villain of such detailed humanity that he has haunted the imaginations of actors and theatre-goers down through the years. Shylock is one of the really great characters of drama and his best-known monument is the phrase he donated to the English language: people who will never hear of Shylock or read this play will understand what it means to want one's *pound of flesh*.

Shylock, of course, was a Jew and anti-Semitism was in fashion when Shakespeare sat down to write his play. Jews were hated especially for their involvement with usury – the practice of taking interest on a loan. Shakespeare's great rival Christopher Marlowe had exploited anti-Jewish feeling in 1590 when he wrote *The Jew of Malta*, a play whose immense popularity was increased in 1594 when Roderigo Lopez – a Jew of Portuguese extraction who was physician to the Queen – was hanged, drawn and quartered at Tyburn, having been convicted (wrongfully as it turned out) of plotting to poison the Queen. There is no doubt that Jewry and its place in the Christian commonwealth would have been a much-debated topic in the taverns of London which Shakespeare frequented. But if Lopez' death gratified some, it also provoked heart-searching in others. Anyone who witnessed his execution, as Shakespeare himself may well have, would have been left in no doubt that if Jews were pricked they would certainly bleed. When Shakespeare sat down to write a rival to Marlowe's popular play, he represented a more circumspect and enlightened attitude although he still geared his play to the interests and moods of an audience who hated Jews.

A lot has changed in four hundred years and the audiences who go to see *The Merchant of Venice* today are very different to those who attended the play's first performances. Usury is no longer the sore point it used to be: in fact the taking of interest is what makes the world go round today. Much more has changed as far as Jews are concerned: if Shylock tells us what it was like to wear the Star of David in the Elizabethan world, the death of six million Jews in the concentration camps of the Third Reich tells what it has been like in our own century. After the Holocaust, things could never be the same again. As W.H. Auden wrote in 1963, *'Recent history has made it utterly impossible for the most unsophisticated and ignorant audience to ignore the historical reality of the Jews and think of them as fairy-story bogeys with huge noses and red wigs.'* ('Brothers and Others' in *The Dyer's Hand*. Faber and Faber Ltd and Random House Inc.) It is not surprising therefore that contemporary theatre companies find greater possibilities in playing Shylock in a more tragic than comic manner.

The question arises perhaps whether this play should be acted at all: some people feel it should be banned; others argue that banning it would simply reflect another kind of totalitarianism and deprive us in the process of a monument to the type of attitudes which eventually led to the Holocaust. It is written at the gates of Auschwitz that those who do not learn from the mistakes of history are condemned to repeat them.

The Merchant of Venice will not comfort us about human nature but its invitation to moral judgement may refine the human nature that is in us. It speaks to us today of outsiders and ghettoised people especially and tells us that if you push people too far they will eventually hit back. It will always be a relevant play for as long as the world has second-class beings and persecuted races, for as long as people are laughed at and especially for as long as a sense of wrong leads to revenge in the form of ferocious acts of terrorism and where pounds of flesh daily splatter the floors of public houses, city streets and airport lounges.

Characters

Antonio	a merchant of Venice.
Bassanio	his friend and suitor to Portia.
Gratiano **Salerio** **Solanio**	friends of Antonio and Bassanio.
Lorenzo	another friend of Antonio and Bassanio who is in love with Jessica.
Shylock	a Jew and moneylender.
Tubal	another Jew, friend of Shylock.
Launcelot Gobbo	a clown, servant to Shylock.
Old Gobbo	father to Launcelot.
Leonardo	servant to Bassanio.
Balthazar **Stephano**	servants to Portia.
Prince of Morocco **Prince of Arragon**	suitors to Portia.
Portia	a rich heiress.
Nerissa	her waiting woman.
Jessica	daughter to Shylock.
Duke of Venice	

Magnificoes of Venice, Officers of the Court of Justice, a Goaler, Servants and other Attendants.

Part 2
Text and Commentary

Act 1

Scene I

Venice. A street. Enter Antonio, Salerio, and Solanio

Antonio

In sooth,[1] I know not why I am so sad:
It wearies me; you say it wearies you;
But how I caught it, found it, or came by it,
What stuff 'tis made of, whereof it is born,
I am to learn;
And such a want-wit[2] sadness makes of me,
That I have much ado[3] to know myself.

I'm sad. I don't know why.

[1] truly

fool (margin note above want-wit)

[2] fool
[3] trouble

Salerio

Your mind is tossing on the ocean,
There, where your argosies[4] with portly[5] sail,
Like signiors[6] and rich burghers[7] on the flood,
Or, as it were, the pageants[8] of the sea,
Do overpeer[9] the petty traffickers,[10]
That curtsy to them, do them reverence,
As they fly by them with their woven wings.

He is concerned about your ships 10

[4] merchant ships
[5] stately
[6] gentleman
[7] rich citizens
[8] floats that were elaborately decorated for festive processions
[9] overlook
[10] small trading boats

Solanio

Believe me, sir, had I such venture[11] forth,
The better part of my affections[12] would
Be with my hopes abroad. I should be still
Plucking the grass to know where sits the wind;
Peering in maps for ports, and piers, and roads;[13]
And every object that might make me fear
Misfortune to my ventures, out of doubt
Would make me sad.

If it was his ships at sea he'd be too worried too

[11] speculative investments
[12] thoughts and feelings

[13] harbours

20

Salerio

        My wind, cooling my broth,[14]
Would blow me to an ague,[15] when I thought
What harm a wind too great might do at sea.
I should not see the sandy hour-glass[16] run
But I should think of shallows and of flats,[17]
And see my wealthy Andrew[18] dock'd in sand
Vailing her high-top lower than her ribs
To kiss her burial. Should I go to church
And see the holy edifice of stone,
And not bethink me straight[19] of dangerous rocks,
Which touching but my gentle vessel's side
Would scatter all her spices on the stream,

Everything then reminds them of the ships
He thinks of the danger for ships

[14] my breath cooling my soup
[15] would send me into a fit of shivering

[16] hour-glass filled with sand
[17] sandbanks
[18] the name of a ship

30

[19] immediately

Enrobe the roaring waters with my silks;
And, in a word, but even now worth this,
And now worth nothing? Shall I have the thought
To think on this, and shall I lack the thought
That such a thing bechanc'd[20] would make me sad?
But tell not me: I know Antonio
Is sad to think upon his merchandise.

Antonio

Believe me, no: I thank my fortune for it,
My ventures are not in one bottom[21] trusted,
Nor to one place; nor is my whole estate
Upon the fortune of this present year:
Therefore, my merchandise makes me not sad.

Solanio

Why, then you are in love.

Antonio

    Fie, fie!

Salerio

Not in love neither? Then let us say you are sad
Because you are not merry: and 'twere as easy
For you to laugh and leap, and say you are merry
Because you are not sad. Now, by two-headed
    Janus,[22]
Nature hath fram'd[23] strange fellows in her time:
Some that will evermore peep through their eyes,
And laugh like parrots at a bag-piper;
And other of such vinegar aspect[24]
That they'll not show their teeth in way of smile,
Though Nestor[25] swear the jest be laughable.

    Enter Bassanio, Lorenzo and Gratiano

Solanio

Here comes Bassanio, your most noble kinsman,
Gratiano, and Lorenzo. Fare ye well:
We leave you now with better company.

Salerio

I would have stay'd till I had made you merry,
If worthier friends had not prevented me.

Antonio

Your worth is very dear in my regard.
I take it, your own business calls on you,
And you embrace th' occasion[26] to depart.

[20]happened

[21]ship

[22]the Roman god of gates and doors had two heads, one facing inwards and the other outwards
[23]made
[24]sour appearance

[25]an old Greek hero who would have been hard to amuse

[26]take the opportunity

40

50

60

Handwritten annotations:
Even if he was in he'd think of the ship.
He knows it's his ships he's worrying about
Everything doesn't rely on ship.
stupid
If there's no reason to be sad then be happy.
Some people are born to be happy some aren't
Here's your friend.
You have lots to do.

4

Salerio

Good morrow, my good lords.

We must get together soon

Bassanio

Good signiors both, when shall we laugh? say,
    when?
You grow exceeding strange: must it be so?

Salerio

We'll make our leisures to attend on yours. ✳ *we'll try*

[*Exeunt Salerio and Solanio*

Lorenzo

My Lord Bassanio, since you have found Antonio,
We two will leave you; but, at dinner-time,   70
I pray you, have in mind where we must meet.

Bassanio

I will not fail you.

Gratiano

You look not well, Signior Antonio;
You have too much respect upon the world:[27]
They lose it that do buy it with much care.[28]
Believe me, you are marvellously chang'd.

Antonio

I hold the world but as the world, Gratiano;
A stage where every man must play a part,
And mine a sad one.

Gratiano

                        Let me play the fool:
With mirth and laughter let old wrinkles come,   80
And let my liver rather heat with wine
Than my heart cool with mortifying groans.
Why should a man, whose blood is warm within,
Sit like his grandsire cut in alabaster?[29]
Sleep when he wakes, and creep into the jaundice
By being peevish? I tell thee what, Antonio—
I love thee, and 'tis my love that speaks—
There are a sort of men whose visages[30]
Do cream and mantle[31] like a standing pond,
And do a wilful stillness entertain,   90
With purpose to be dress'd in an opinion[33]
Of wisdom, gravity, profound conceit,
As who should say, 'I am Sir Oracle,[34]
And when I ope my lips, let no dog bark!'
O my Antonio, I do know of these

[27] you worry too much about the world
[28] worry does not bring success or happiness

[29] be like a statue

[30] faces
[31] stagnate
[32] adopt a deliberate air of solemnity
[33] to get a reputation for
[34] wise as the Greek oracle: the oracle's voice was inspired by the gods

That therefore only are reputed wise
For saying nothing; when, I am very sure,
If they should speak, would almost damn those ears
Which, hearing them, would call their brothers fools.
I'll tell thee more of this another time: *100*
But fish not, with this melancholy bait,[35]
For this fool-gudgeon,[36] this opinion.
Come, good Lorenzo. Fare ye well awhile:
I'll end my exhortation [37] after dinner.

Lorenzo

Well, we will leave you then till dinner-time.
I must be one of these same dumb wise men,
For Gratiano never lets me speak.

Gratiano

Well, keep me company but two years more,
Thou shalt not know the sound of thine own tongue.

Antonio

Fare you well: I'll grow a talker for this gear.[38]   *110*

Gratiano

Thanks, i' faith; for silence is only commendable
In a neat's tongue dried[39] and a maid not vendible[40]

[Exeunt Gratiano and Lorenzo

Antonio

Is that anything now?

Bassanio

Gratiano speaks an infinite deal of nothing, more than
any man in all Venice. His reasons are as two grains of
wheat hid in two bushels of chaff: you shall seek all
day ere you find them, and when you have them, they
are not worth the search.

Antonio

Well, tell me now, what lady is the same
To whom you swore a secret pilgrimage,   *120*
 That you today promis'd to tell me of?

Tell me this about you girl you went to see.

Bassanio

'Tis not unknown to you, Antonio,
How much I have disabled mine estate,[41]
By something showing a more swelling port[42]
Than my faint means would grant continuamce[43]
Nor do I now make moan to be abridg'd[44]
From such a noble rate; but my chief care
Is, to come fairly off[45] from the great debts

I have spent all my money.

[35]do not use sadness to gain attention
[36]stupid fish

[37]sermon

[38]as a result of this nonsense

[39]preserved ox-tongue
[40]that cannot be married

[41]squandered my money
[42]opulent lifestyle
[43]than my slender income would allow
[44]complain about cutbacks

[45]to get out of

Wherein my time, something too prodigal,[46]
Hath left me gag'd.[47] To you, Antonio,
I owe the most, in money and in love;
And from your love I have a warranty[48]
To unburden all my plots and purposes
How to get clear of all the debts I owe.

[handwritten: Want to pay back what I owe. Because he's been a good friend he'll tell him how to pay back]

130

[46]extravagant
[47]in debt

[48]licence

Antonio

I pray you, good Bassanio, let me know it;
And if it stand, as you yourself still do,
Within the eye of honour, be assur'd,
My purse, my person, my extremest means,
Lie all unlock'd to your occasions.[49]

[handwritten: I'll give anything to Bassanio]

[49]are at your disposal

Bassanio

In my school-days, when I had lost one shaft,[50]
I shot his fellow of the self-same flight [51]
The self-same way with more advised[52] watch,
To find the other forth; and by adventuring both,
I oft found both. I urge[53] this childhood proof,[54]
Because what follows is pure innocence.
I owe you much, and (like a wilful youth)
That which I owe is lost; but if you please
To shoot another arrow that self way
Which you did shoot the first, I do not doubt,
(As I will watch the aim) or to find both,
Or bring your latter hazard[55] back again,
And thankfully rest debtor[56] for the first.

[handwritten: You've given me money and I lost it. But if you give me more I'll give it all back]

140

150

[50]arrow
[51]an identical arrow
[52]careful

[53]offer
[54]illustration

[55]the latest loan you have risked
[56]remain in debt

Antonio

You know me well, and herein spend but time
To wind about my love with circumstance;[57]
And out of doubt you do me now more wrong
In making question of my uttermost [58]
Than if you had made waste of all I have.
Then do but say to me what I should do
That in your knowledge may by me be done,
And I am prest unto it: therefore speak.

[handwritten: Your insulting me by doubting I'd give you be money what I'll do what I can to help.]

160

[57]to beat about the bush

[58]in doubting that I would do my best

Bassanio

In Belmont is a lady richly left,[59]
And she is fair, and, fairer than her word,
Of wondrous virtues: sometimes from her eyes
I did receive fair speechless[60] messages:
Her name is Portia; nothing undervalu'd[61]
To Cato's daughter, Brutus' Portia;
Nor is the wide world ignorant of her worth,

[59]who has inherited great wealth

[60]unspoken
[61]not inferior

For the four winds blow in from every coast
Renowned suitors; and her sunny locks
Hang on her temples like a golden fleece;
Which makes her seat of Belmont Colchis' strand,   170
And many Jasons come in quest of her.[62]
O my Antonio, had I but the means
To hold a rival place with one of them,
I have a mind presages me such thrift [63]
That I should questionless [64] be fortunate.

He'll marry Portia and then pay back Antonio.

Antonio

Thou know'st that all my fortunes are at sea;
Neither have I money, nor commodity[65]
To raise a present sum: therefore go forth,
Try what my credit can in Venice do: 180
That shall be rack'd,[66] even to the uttermost,
To furnish[67] thee to Belmont, to fair Portia.
Go, presently[68] inquire, and so will I,
Where money is, and I no question make
To have it of my trust or for my sake.

[Exeunt

[62] in Greek mythology Jason made a voyage to Colchis in search of the golden fleece
[63] promises me such financial success
[64] undoubtedly
[65] merchandise which could be offered as security for a loan
[66] stretched
[67] to be fitted out for
[68] at once

Summary

Antonio's Mysterious Sadness

The play opens on a street in Venice where Antonio, a great Venetian merchant, is explaining to two friends, Salerio and Solanio, that he is inexplicably sad. They suggest that his anxiety is understandable since his ships at sea are at the mercy of the weather. Antonio rejects this explanation of his depression on the grounds that he does not have all his eggs in one basket. A further suggestion arises, that he is possibly in love; this he rejects out of hand.

As the mystified Salerio and Solanio resort to humour in an effort to cheer up Antonio, they are joined by Lorenzo, Gratiano and Bassanio, the latter of whom we understand to be a close friend of Antonio. As Salerio and Solanio leave, Gratiano scolds Antonio for his depressed appearance and tries in turn to humour him. He ends up accusing Antonio of putting it on for effect and suggests he had better pull himself together.

Gratiano and Lorenzo go to dinner, leaving Bassanio and Antonio alone. Bassanio confesses that he has spent a great deal of money, much of it borrowed from Antonio who reassures him nevertheless of continued generosity.

Bassanio has now fallen in love with Portia, a rich and beautiful heiress, but feels he hasn't the means to compete for her affections. Antonio has no cash available at the moment; he has invested all his assets in a merchant fleet. He promises, however, to help Bassanio borrow from moneylenders so that Bassanio can go to Belmont to visit Portia.

Scene Analysis

The Background And Atmosphere Against Which The Story Begins

An opening scene is always important: it establishes the background and very often the atmosphere of a play, gets the action or plot underway and gives us a first impression of the characters it introduces.

I hold the world but as the world, Gratiano;
A stage where every man must play a part,
And mine a sad one.   (Antonio, Act 1, Sc I)

Background

The background here is Venice, a rich maritime trading city whose glory had declined by the 1590s but whose reputation remained synonymous with the culture, luxury and wealth to which the Elizabethans aspired. We get a sense of the place in the elegant and colourful language of Antonio's friends:

'There, where your argosies with portly sail,
Like signiors and rich burghers on the flood,
Or, as it were, the pageants of the sea,
Do overpeer the petty traffickers,'

Atmosphere

Imposing itself on this scene is the gloomy mood in which we find Antonio. It is a mood which is emphasised by the contrasting good humour of his friends. In contrast to his friends' elegant and colourful language, Antonio's words are direct and depressed:

'...I know not why I am so sad:'

These words not only arouse our suspense but also a feeling of vulnerability and fragility:

'...how I caught it, found it, or came by it,
What stuff 'tis made of, whereof it is born,
I am to learn;'

Is it, we wonder, the shadow of coming events?

The element of unease is reinforced by the images of 'dangerous rocks' and 'roaring waters' so ready on the lips of Antonio's friends. Sea and tempest symbolise external forces over which man has no control. We can see clearly that the destruction of his vessels would ruin Antonio.

The Story Begins

Having aroused our suspense, Shakespeare immerses us deftly into the anxieties we will have to entertain before the final happy ever after of Romantic Comedy. Will Bassanio get his money and how, and what will become of Antonio? (the bond story). Who will win the hand of 'fair Portia'?(the casket story). What, we wonder, will happen next?

Characters

ANTONIO

Rich, Depressed And Generous

Antonio is the great and rich 'Merchant of Venice' of the play's title. His depression puzzles his friends as it has puzzled generations of scholars. It even puzzles Antonio himself:

'...I have much ado to know myself.'

He is not usually as despondent however as we find him here.

'Believe me,' Gratiano tells him, 'you are marvellously chang'd.'

Being a man of property, Antonio's depression is easily interpreted as having:

'...too much respect upon the world:'

But Antonio is not obsessed with his investments, and wealth has not gone to his head:

'I hold the world but as a world, Gratiano;
A stage where every man must play a part
And mine a sad one.'

That Antonio is sincere in these remarks is proved by his remarkable and extravagant generosity to Bassanio.

'...be assur'd,
My purse, my person, my extremest means,
Lie all unlock'd to your occasions.'

It is a boundless generosity which makes him very vulnerable. Antonio is not just an easy touch where friends and money are concerned, he is a man who will put his very life in jeopardy for a friend.

BASSANIO

Is He A Fortune Hunter?

Although Bassanio enters the scene with a 'most noble' reputation, our first impressions of him are generally unfavourable. He strikes us as an improvident fortune hunter who, having benefited from Antonio's generosity in the past, now asks him to throw good money after bad.

'That which I owe is lost; but if you please
To shoot another arrow that self way...'

His 'chief care' is 'How to get clear of all the debts I owe.' To this end he has 'plots and purposes' to share with Antonio. He has a business proposition, and her name is Portia.

'In Belmont is a lady richly left,'

He is quite obviously enraptured:

'And she is fair, and, fairer than that word,
Of wondrous virtues:'

But if Bassanio is in love with Portia, is it not strange that his language is so laced with calculation?

'nothing undervalu'd... her worth'!

Genuine images of love are so fused with images of richness that even her hair is a 'golden fleece'.

What then are we to make of this prospective suitor for Portia? Has he any saving grace other than his openess? Our initial impression should be tempered by two points of information:

(a) The tradition of the play directs that Bassanio be a dazzling charmer in bearing and in costume, so handsome as to be deemed irresistable.

(b) The Elizabethans set great importance on a dowry and approved of fortune hunting. Shakespeare's first audience would not have frowned on Bassanio for a moment.

We shall see if he will redeem himself with us.

PORTIA

A Dazzling Reputation

Although we do not meet Portia in this scene, we learn a lot about her reputation. She is *'fair'* and *'richly left'* and of *'wondrous virtues'*. She is consequently very sought-after and

> *'... the four winds blow in from every coast*
> *Renowned suitors;'*

We are anxious to meet her ourselves.

Minor Characters

GRATIANO

Gratiano is cast as the wit of the company, an irrepressible buffoon who cannot fathom those less happily extroverted than himself.

> *'Why should a man, whose blood is warm within,*
> *Sit like his grandsire cut in alabaster?'*

Although he is well-meaning and sincere:

> *'I love thee, and 'tis my love that speaks...'*

Antonio and Bassanio agree that he speaks:

> *'an infinite deal of nothing...'*

SALERIO AND SOLANIO

Salero and Solanio are two very undefined characters who are just about as distinguishable as their names. Their light-heartedness serves merely to underline Antonio's gloom.

Scene II

Belmont. A room in Portia's house. Enter Portia, and Nerissa

Portia

By my troth,[1] Nerissa, my little body is aweary[2] *By God, I'm weary*
of this great world.

Nerissa

You would be, sweet madam, if your miseries were in *Cheer up! Look at all you have.*
the same abundance as your good fortunes are: and
yet, for aught I see, they are as sick that surfeit[3] with *people who have too much aren't*
too much as they that starve with nothing. It is no
mean happiness therefore, to be seated in the mean[4]: *much as happy.*
superfluity[5] comes sooner by white hairs, but
competency[6] lives longer.

[1] faith
[2] tired
[3] eat to excess
[4] middle
[5] having too much
[6] having just enough

Portia

Good sentences, and well pronounced.   10

Nerissa

They would be better if well followed.

Portia

If to do were as easy as to know what were good to *It's easier to tell people what to do than to do it yourself.*
do, chapels had been churches, and poor men's
cottages princes' palaces. It is a good divine[7] that
follows his own instructions: I can easier teach twenty
what were good to be done, than be one of the twenty *It's not fair*
to follow mine own teaching. The brain may devise *that I can't choose my*
laws for the blood,[8] but a hot temper leaps o'er a
cold decree: such a hare is madness (the youth),
to skip o'er the meshes of good counsel[9] (the *own   20*
cripple). But this reasoning is not in the fashion to *husband*
choose me a husband. O me, the word 'choose'! I
may neither choose who I would nor refuse who I
dislike; so is the will of a living daughter curbed[10] by
the will of a dead father. Is it not hard, Nerissa, that I
cannot choose one, nor refuse none?

[7] preacher
[8] one's passions
[9] advice
[10] restrained

Nerissa

Your father was ever virtuous, and holy men at their
death have good inspirations; therefore, the lottery
that he hath devised in these three chests of gold,
silver, and lead, whereof who chooses his meaning   30
chooses you, will, no doubt, never be chosen by any
rightly but one who you shall rightly love. But what

Your dad had your best interests at heart

warmth is there in your affection towards any of these
princely suitors that are already come?   *what do you think*
Portia   *of the people who have already*
I pray thee, over-name them,[11] and as thou namest   *come?*
them, I will describe them; and, according to my
description, level[12] at my affection.

[11]go over their names

[12]guess

Nerissa

First there is the Neapolitan prince.

Portia

Ay, that's a colt indeed, for he doth nothing but talk of
his horse; and he makes it a great appropriation[13]   40
to his own good parts that he can shoe him himself. I
am much afeard my lady his mother played false with
a smith.   *He talks too much about his horses.*

[13]accomplishment

Nerissa

Then is there the County Palatine.

Portia

He doth nothing but frown, as who should say, 'And
you will not have me, choose.' He hears merry tales,
and smiles not: I fear he will prove the weeping
philosopher when he grows old, being so full of
unmannerly sadness in his youth. I had rather be
married to a death's-head[14] with a bone in his   50
mouth than to either of these. God defend me from
these two!   *Nothing makes him happy. He's too*
                                                           sad.

[14]skull

Nerissa

How say you by the French lord, Monsieur Le Bon?

Portia

God made him, and therefore let him pass for a man.
In truth, I know it is a sin to be mocker; but, he! why,
he hath a horse better than the Neapolitan's, a better
bad habit of frowning than the Count Palatine; he is
every man in no man; if a throstle[15] sing, he falls
straight a-capering; he will fence with his own
shadow. If I should marry him, I should marry twenty   60
husbands: if he would despise me, I would forgive
him, for if he loves me to madness, I shall never
requite[16] him.   *He has everyones faults.*

[15]thrush

[16]return his love

Nerissa

What say you, then, to Falconbridge, the young baron
of England?

Portia

You know I say nothing to him, for he understands not
me, nor I him: he hath neither Latin, French, nor
Italian; and you will come into the court and swear
that I have a poor pennyworth[17] in the English. He is a
proper man's picture, but, alas! who can converse   70
with a dumb-show? How oddly he is suited! I think he
bought his doublet[18] in Italy, his round hose[19] in
France, his bonnet in Germany, and his behaviour
everywhere.

[17] not very much

[18] tunic
[19] stockings or breeches

Nerissa

What think you of the Scottish lord, his neighbour?

Portia

That he hath a neighbourly charity in him, for he
borrowed a box[20] of the ear of the Englishman, and
swore he would pay him again when he was able: I
think the Frenchman became his surety[21] and sealed
under[22] for another.   80

[20] blow

[21] guaranteed that the debt
     would be repaid
[22] signed his name

Nerissa

How like you the young German, the Duke of Saxony's
nephew?

Portia

Very vilely in the morning, when he is sober, and most
vilely in the afternoon, when he is drunk: when he is
best, he is a little worse than a man, and when he is
worst, he is little better than a beast. And the worst
fall that ever fell, I hope I shall make shift[23] to go
without him.

[23] manage to

Nerissa

If he should offer to choose, and choose the right
casket, you should refuse to perform your father's   90
will, if you should refuse to accept him.

Portia

Therefore, for fear of the worst, I pray thee, set a deep
glass of Rhenish wine[24] on the contrary[25] casket, for,
if the devil be within and that temptation
without, I know he will choose it. I will do anything,
Nerissa, ere I will be married to a sponge.

[24] wine from the Rhine
     Valley
[25] wrong

Nerissa

You need not fear, lady, the having any of these lords:
they have acquainted me with their determinations;
which is, indeed, to return to their home and to
trouble you with no more suit, unless you may be   100

won by some other sort than your father's imposition depending on the caskets.

Portia

26 a prophetess in classical mythology who was granted long life by Apollo
27 the Roman goddess of virginity and light

If I live to be as old as Sibylla,[26] I will die as chaste as Diana,[27] unless I be obtained by the manner of my father's will. I am glad this parcel of wooers are so reasonable, for there is not one among them but I dote on his very absence, and I pray God grant them a fair departure.

Nerissa

Do you not remember, lady, in your father's time, a Venetian, a scholar and a soldier, that came hither in company of the Marquis of Montferrat?

Do you remember a student and soldier. 110

Portia

Yes, yes: it was Bassanio — as I think so was he called.

Nerissa

True, madam: he of all the men that ever my foolish eyes looked upon, was the best deserving a fair lady.

he's the best so far

Portia

I remember him well, and I remember him worthy of thy praise.

Enter a Servant

How now, what news?

Servant

The four strangers seek for you, madam, to take their leave; and there is a forerunner come from a fifth, the Prince of Morocco, who brings word the prince his master will be here tonight.

120

The prince of Morocco is coming

Portia

If I could bid the fifth welcome with so good heart as I can bid the other four farewell, I should be glad of his approach: if he have the condition of a saint and the complexion of a devil, I had rather he should shrive[28] me than wive[29] me.

I'm so happy they are leaving. I wish could be happy they arrive.

28 hear my confession
29 marry
30 a way of addressing a servant

Come, Nerissa. *[To Attendant]* Sirrah,[30] go before. Whiles we shut the gate upon one wooer, another knocks at the door.

One goes another comes.

[Exeunt

130

Summary

A Husband For Portia

In Belmont, Portia like Antonio is despondent and Nerissa her companion reminds her of her good fortune. Nerissa points out that too much wealth can be as much a barrier to happiness as poverty. Portia agrees but rejoins that it is easier to preach sermons than to live by them. She feels hard done by in being deprived of choice as to who her husband will be by the terms of her father's will. Only the man who chooses the right one in a lottery of three caskets will win Portia's hand.

Portia and Nerissa now begin a review of the suitors who have thus far appeared. Nerissa names them and Portia dismisses them one by one. One is preoccupied with horses; one is much too serious; one is too wishy-washy; another is inept at continental languages and dresses oddly; another still is too canny; yet another is a drunkard.

Portia despises them all but will be governed by her father's will. However, the suitors who are currently courting Portia are so discouraged by her cold shoulder and so daunted by the risk of failure that they depart without further ado.

Nerissa finally reminds Portia of Bassanio and he alone of all the suitors is considered favourably. The scene ends as Portia prepares without enthusiasm for the arrival of yet another suitor, the Prince of Morocco.

Scene Analysis

Scene II introduces us to Belmont, to Portia and to comedy while carrying on the story a stage further.

Belmont

Belmont is a charmed and enchanted world which contrasts starkly with the cold business world of Venice. It is a fairy-tale setting where romance is a game involving caskets and where a father can devise the most ridiculous method of finding a husband for his daughter.

Portia Introduced

Our curiosity has been aroused about the lady of Belmont and now she is introduced to us as *'a living daughter curbed by the will of a dead father.'*

Comedy

Comedy flourishes not so much in spite of but because of the *'inspirations'* of Portia's father. In a scene that would have been rich in entertainment for an Elizabethan audience, Portia wittily exposes the national characteristics of her suitors. The Neapolitans were renowned for their skill with horses:

'he doth nothing but talk of his horse.'

The French were famous for their gestures:

'he will fence with his own shadow.'

The Germans were drunkards, the Scots crafty, and so on.

With good-humoured impartiality, Shakespeare extends his satire to include his audience. Portia pokes fun at the English for their renowned linguistic ineptitude:

'he hath neither Latin, French, nor Italian...'

An airing of the reputed rivalry between the Scots and the English was also calculated to rouse a cheer from the pit:

'for he borrowed a box of the ear of the Englishman...'

I may neither choose who I would nor refuse who I dislike; so is the will of a living daughter curbed by the will of a dead father.   (Portia, Act 1, Sc II)

The Story Continues

Having told us something of the device of the caskets upon which so much is to depend, Shakespeare allows us to glean, from a suddenly wistful Portia, that Bassanio has made a favourable impression. Tension persists, however, for since Portia will be governed by her father's will, Bassanio's chances of gaining her hand depend on his choosing the right casket and his doing so before anyone else.

Characters

PORTIA

Pampered But Unspoiled

If Portia is as *'richly left'* as Bassanio says she is, she is not correspondingly happy:

> *'my little body is aweary of this great world.'*

Portia's problem is that her wealth has come with strings attached: she is *'curbed'* by the strictures of her father's will. *'Is it not hard'* she asks Nerissa that she *'cannot choose one, nor refuse none'.*

Portia's saving grace is that she does not take herself or her problems too seriously. Yes, she can be serious and circumspect when the occasion demands:

> *'It is a good divine that follows his own instructions:'*

but she can be extremely witty as well. Of her *'parcel of wooers',* she says,

> *'...there is not one among them but I dote on his very absence.'*

There is a formidable sharpness to the humour with which she dismisses her suitors. Is it, we wonder, the brilliant flippancy of the over-indulged? The tone of her speech and her egalitarian treatment of Nerissa suggest otherwise. Her witty sallies are exuberantly light-hearted and reflect what appears to be a delightfully competent intellect full of vitality, resilience and incision.

NERISSA

Confidential Companion

Nerissa is not so much a maid as a confidential companion to Portia. We notice the freedom and confidence with which Portia discusses very personal things with her: her father's will and her various suitors.

Nerissa is not, however, over-familiar. She addresses Portia with terms that display both affection and respect: *'sweet madam'* and *'lady'.*

Portia and Nerissa are well-matched both in shrewdness and in wit. Indeed it is open to question which of them is the better philosopher. Portia has to admit that sentiments such as:

> *'...they are as sick that surfeit with too much as they that starve with nothing.'*

are: *'Good sentences, and well pronounced.'*

We notice for ourselves the knowing sublety about the way Nerissa raises the question of Bassanio:

> 'Do you not remember, lady, in your father's time, a Venetian, a scholar and a soldier, that came hither...?'

We remember Nerissa best from this scene, however, for the keen and impish pleasure she takes in drawing out Portia's comments on the various suitors:

> 'What say you, then, to Falconbridge, the young baron of England?'

Scene III

Venice. A public place. Enter Bassanio, and Shylock

Shylock
Three thousand ducats;[1] well.

Bassanio
Ay, sir, for three months.

Shylock
For three months; well.

Bassanio
For the which, as I told you, Antonio shall be bound.[2]

Shylock
Antonio shall become bound; well.

Bassanio
May you stead[3] me? Will you pleasure me? Shall I
know your answer?

Shylock
Three thousand ducats, for three months, and
Antonio bound.

Bassanio
Your answer to that?   10

Shylock
Antonio is a good man.

Bassanio
Have you heard any imputation[4] to the contrary?

Shylock
Ho, no, no, no, no; my meaning in saying he is a good
man is to have you understand me that he is
sufficient.[5] Yet his means are in supposition:[6]
he hath an argosy[7] bound to Tripolis, another to the

[1] Venetian coin

[2] guarantor

[3] supply

[4] charge

[5] solvent, financially
   adequate
[6] in doubt
[7] ship

Indies; I understand moreover, upon the Rialto,[8] he
hath a third at Mexico, a fourth for England, and other
ventures he hath squandered abroad. But ships are
but boards, sailors but men: there be land-rats and   20
water-rats, water-thieves and land-thieves — I mean
pirates — and then there is the peril of waters, winds,
and rocks. The man is, notwithstanding, sufficient.
Three thousand ducats; I think I may take his bond.

Bassanio

Be assured you may.

Shylock

I will be assured I may; and, that I may be assured,
I will bethink me. May I speak with Antonio?

Bassanio

If it please you to dine with us.

Shylock

Yes, to smell pork; to eat of the habitation which your
prophet the Nazarite[9] conjured the devil into. I will   30
buy with you, sell with you, talk with you, walk with
you, and so following; but I will not eat with you, drink
with you, nor pray with you. What news on the Rialto?
Who is he comes here?

Enter Antonio

Bassanio

This is Signior Antonio.

Shylock

*[Aside]*How like a fawning[10] publican[11] he looks!
I hate him for he is a Christian;
But more for that in low simplicity
He lends out money gratis,[12] and brings down
The rate of usance[13] here with us in Venice.   40
If I can catch him once upon the hip,[14]
I will feed fat the ancient grudge I bear him.
He hates our sacred nation, and he rails,[15]
Even there where merchants most do congregate,
On me, my bargains, and my well-won thrift,
Which he calls interest. Cursed be my tribe,
If I forgive him!

Bassanio

       Shylock, do you hear?

[8] the Venetian Stock
Exchange

[9] Jesus Christ

[10] cringing, servile
[11] tax collector or innkeeper

[12] free of charge
[13] interest

[14] at a disadvantage

[15] abuses

(handwritten annotations: Doesn't change interest; get revenge, shouts over Shylock at Market)

Shylock

I am debating of my present store,[16]
And, by the near guess of my memory,
I cannot instantly raise up the gross   50
Of full three thousand ducats. What of that?
Tubal, a wealthy Hebrew of my tribe,
Will furnish[17] me. But soft! how many months
Do you desire! *[To Antonio]* Rest you fair, good
    signior;
Your worship was the last man in our mouths.

Antonio

Shylock, albeit[18] I neither lend nor borrow
By taking nor by giving of excess,
Yet, to supply the ripe[19] wants of my friend,
I'll break a custom. *[To Bassanio]* Is he yet
            possess'd[20]
How much ye would?[21]   60

Shylock

                    Ay, ay, three thousand ducats.

Antonio

And for three months.

Shylock

I had forgot; three months; you told me so.
Well then, your bond; and let me see — but hear you;
Methought[22] you said, you neither lend nor borrow
Upon advantage.[23]

Antonio

        I do never use it.

Drawing it out to make Bassanio uncomfortable.

Shylock

When Jacob graz'd his uncle Laban's sheep[24] —
This Jacob from our holy Abram was,
As his wise mother wrought in his behalf,
The third possessor: ay, he was the third —

Antonio

And what of him? did he take interest?   70

Shylock

No, not take interest; not, as you would say,
Directly interest: mark what Jacob did.
When Laban and himself were compromis'd,[25]
That all the eanlings[26] which were streak'd and pied[27]
Should fall as Jacob's hire,[28] the ewes, being rank,[29]
In end of autumn turned to the rams;

Side notes:

[16] money
[17] supply
[18] although
[19] urgent
[20] informed of
[21] you want
[22] I thought
[23] where interest was charged
[24] a story from the Book of Genesis
[25] had reached an agreement
[26] lambs
[27] spotted
[28] wages
[29] ready for mating

And, when the work of generation was
Between these woolly breeders in the act,
The skilful shepherd pill'd me certain wands.[30]
And, in the doing of the deed of kind,[31]   80
He stuck them up before the fulsome[32] ewes,
Who, then conceiving, did in eaning[33] time
Fall[34] parti-colour'd lambs, and those were Jacob's.
This was a way to thrive, and he was blest:
And thrift is blessing, if men steal it not.

Antonio

This was a venture, sir, that Jacob serv'd for;
A thing not in his power to bring to pass,
But sway'd and fashion'd by the hand of heaven.
Was this inserted to make interest good?
Or is your gold and silver ewes and rams?   90

Shylock

I cannot tell; I make it breed as fast:
But note me, signior.

Antonio

                    Mark you this, Bassanio,
The devil can cite[35] Scripture for his purpose.
An evil soul, producing holy witness,
Is like a villain with a smiling cheek,
A goodly apple rotten at the heart.
O what a goodly outside falsehood hath!

very disgusted at Shylock

Shylock

Three thousand ducats; 'tis a good round sum.
Three months from twelve: then, let me see, the rate —

Antonio

ignores anger

Well, Shylock, shall we be beholding[36] to you?   100

Shylock

Signior Antonio, many a time and oft
In the Rialto you have rated[37] me
About my moneys and my usances.[38]
Still have I borne it with a patient shrug,
For sufferance[39] is the badge of all our tribe.
You call me misbeliever, cut-throat dog,
And spit upon my Jewish gaberdine,[40]
And all for use of that which is mine own.
Well then, it now appears you need my help:
Go to[41] then; you come to me, and you say,
'Shylock, we would have moneys:' you say so;   110
You, that did void your rheum[42] upon my beard,

hasn't said anything about insults

humiliation

[30]stripped the bark from
 some twigs
[31]coition
[32]passionate
[33]lambing
[34]gave birth to

[35]quote

[36]obliged, indebted

[37]abused
[38]interest taking

[39]patience

[40]coat

[41]'come off it then'

[42]spit

23

⁴³kick
⁴⁴dog
⁴⁵what you seek

⁴⁶the tone of a slave

⁴⁷take interest from money

⁴⁸a Dutch coin of little value
⁴⁹interest

⁵⁰solicitor

⁵¹penalty for breaking an
  agreement

And foot[43] me as you spurn a stranger cur[44]
Over your threshold. Moneys is your suit[45]
What should I say to you? Should I not say,
'Hath a dog money? Is it possible
A cur can lend three thousand ducats?' or
Shall I bend low, and in a bondman's key,[46]
With bated breath, and whispering humbleness,
Say this:
'Fair sir, you spat on me on Wednesday last;
You spurn'd me such a day; another time
You call'd me dog — and for these courtesies
I'll lend you thus much moneys'?

Antonio

I am as like to call thee so again,
To spit on thee again, to spurn thee too.
If thou wilt lend this money, lend it not
As to thy friends, for when did friendship take
A breed for barren metal[47] of his friend?
But lend it rather to thine enemy;
Who if he break, thou may'st with better face
Exact the penalty.

Shylock

         Why, look you, how you storm!
I would be friends with you, and have your love,
Forget the shames that you have stain'd me with,
Supply your present wants, and take no doit[48]
Of usance[49] for my moneys, and you'll not hear me:
This is kind I offer.

Bassanio

This were kindness.

Shylock

      This kindness will I show.
Go with me to a notary,[50] seal me there
Your single bond; and, in a merry sport,
If you repay me not on such a day,
In such a place, such sum or sums as are
Express'd in the condition, let the forfeit[51]
Be nominated for an equal pound
Of your fair flesh, to be cut off and taken
In what part of your body pleaseth me.

Antonio

Content, in faith: I'll seal to such a bond,
And say there is much kindness in the Jew.

120

130

140

Bassanio

You shall not seal to such a bond for me:
I'll rather dwell in my necessity.   *150*

Antonio

Why, fear not, man, I will not forfeit it:
Within these two months, that's a month before
This bond expires, I do expect return
Of thrice three times the value of this bond.

Shylock

O father Abram, what these Christians are,
Whose own hard dealings teaches them suspect
The thoughts of others! Pray you, tell me this:
If he should break his day, what should I gain
By the exaction of the forfeiture?
A pound of man's flesh, taken from a man,   *160*
Is not so estimable,[52] profitable neither,   [52]possible to value
As flesh of muttons, beefs, or goats. I say,
To buy his favour, I extend this friendship:
If he will take it, so; if not, adieu;
And, for my love, I pray you wrong me not.

Antonio

Yes, Shylock, I will seal unto this bond.

Shylock

Then meet me forthwith at the notary's;
Give him direction for this merry bond.
And I will go and purse the ducats straight,[53]   [53]immediately
See to my house, left in the fearful guard   *170*
Of an unthrifty knave,[54] and presently   [54]a careless fellow
I'll be with you.

                                        [Exit Shylock

Antonio

        Hie thee, gentle Jew.
The Hebrew will turn Christian: he grows kind.

Bassanio

I like not fair terms and a villain's mind.

Antonio

Come on: in this there can be no dismay;
My ships come home a month before the day.

                                        [Exeunt

Summary

Shylock The Moneylender

Back in Venice, Bassanio has sought out the moneylender Shylock and is citing Antonio as guarantor for his proposed borrowing. Shylock mulls over Antonio's credit rating and requests a meeting. Bassanio proposes a business lunch but Shylock will not dine with Christians. An impasse is avoided when Antonio arrives there and then. In an aside full of concentrated venom, Shylock expresses a deep hatred for Antonio both because he is a Christian and because he lends money without charging interest, thus reducing the prevailing rate chargeable by moneylenders such as Shylock. We also gather from Shylock that Antonio has treated him very badly in the past and that Shylock is on the lookout for an opportunity to settle old scores.

A discussion arises about the whole question of usury – the taking of interest on a loan. It is a practice which Antonio – though party to borrowing now – normally opposes. Shylock justifies usury by citing the Old Testament story of how Jacob profited by his skill in sheep breeding. Antonio argues that Jacob's fortune was the result of the will of God and was not consequently comparable to usury.

The argument reaches a standstill and Shylock complains bitterly at the way Antonio used to spit on him and call him a dog. Antonio does not propose to amend his ways but is disarmed suddenly when Shylock offers to let bygones be bygones and to give an interest-free loan of the money required as a token of friendship. Shylock, however, adds one condition as a kind of joke – that a bond be entered into, whereby, if Antonio cannot repay the sum within a stipulated three months, he must forfeit a pound of his own flesh.

Although Bassanio has misgivings, Antonio has been softened by Shylock's gesture and will sign the bond, confident in the timely return of his ships.

Scene Analysis

This scene offers a strong contrast to the previous scene. It introduces us to the only major character we have yet to meet and raises the tension of the drama as it moves the plot onwards.

Contrast

Scene III takes us away from the enchanted land of Belmont and shows us another side of the world we are dealing with. We are back in the harsh mercantile world of Venice with its racial and religious tensions, malicious talk, sly tactics and hard bargaining. The scene's first words are about money:

'Three thousand ducats; well.'

The rasping voice is that of Shylock whose character henceforth dominates the play.

The Villain Introduced

Shylock represented to an Elizabethan audience two of the things they most abhorred: Jewry and usury.

Jews had been officially expelled from England since 1290 and they would not regain civil rights until centuries after this play was written. Forbidden to trade or hold a profession, they turned to lending money and charging interest on it. The rates of interest were usually exorbitant. Antonio voices not only the audience's centuries-old prejudice and superstition towards Jews, but also the resentment and hostility of people who in many instances found themselves in debt to Jewish moneylenders.

Fair sir, you spat on me on Wednesday last;
You spurn'd me such a day; another time
You call'd me dog — and for these courtesies
I'll lend you thus much moneys?   *(Shylock, Act 1, Sc III)*

The Drama Intensifies

The tension which pervades this scene has its chief source in Shylock. He is, as it were, the cat among the pigeons. His talk of *'the peril of waters, winds, and rocks'* touches a nerve sensitised in Scene I. The threat becomes explicit when in a voice full of ensnaring venom he says of Antonio:

> *'If I can catch him once upon the hip,*
> *I will feed fat the ancient grudge I bear him.'*

And like any cat among pigeons, we cannot take our eyes off him, fearful of what he will do next. What, we wonder, is he up to? Is he out to humiliate Antonio into taking charity from an enemy? Or, is it the outside chance of taking Antonio's life that he is angling for? Could he possibly be trying to make friends with an old enemy?

The sheer length of time it takes Shylock to answer Bassanio's question *'May you stead me?'* sustains suspense and contributes to our unease. But even when Shylock finally answers, our unease does not go away. Bassanio's parting words are laden with foreboding:

> *'I like not fair terms and a villain's mind.'*

The scene ends on a note of dramatic irony as Antonio tempts fate:

> *'My ships come home a month before the day.'*

The Plot Moves Onwards

Scene III completes the exposition of the two main plot lines in the play. The casket story was introduced in Scene II and now the bond story is set in motion as Antonio agrees that if he cannot repay Shylock by the appointed time he must forfeit *'an equal pound'* of his *'fair flesh'*.

Characters

SHYLOCK

Villain Or Victim

Having established Shylock's dramatic effect upon the scene, we can now look a little more closely at his character, at what flesh and bones accrue to a stock Jewish villain in the hands of a great dramatist.

Shylock's initial impact does nothing to question an audience clear in its mind that this Jewish moneylender is a villain. Villains must be inhuman in some way and traditionally Shylock's dress and deportment (a huge hooked nose, gaberdine coat, a red wig and beard) produce theatrically a dehumanising effect which is heightened by the fragmented monotone of his parrot-like speech:

> *'Three thousand ducats; well...'*
> *'For three months; well...'*
> *'Antonio shall be bound; well...'*

Shylock is dehumanised morally by his amoral equation of goodness and financial adequacy.

> *'...my meaning in saying he is a good*
> *man is to have you understand me that he is*
> *sufficient.'*

Nothing will dehumanise Shylock, however, as much as his so-called *'merry bond'*. If he is really out for a pound of Antonio's flesh, then he is truly beyond the pale.

On the other hand, we cannot say that Shylock's hatred for Antonio is unprovoked. Antonio has publicly undermined Shylock on his own ground:

> *'You call me misbeliever, cut-throat dog,*
> *And spit upon my Jewish gaberdine,'*

Modern audiences do not share the anti-Semitism of the play's first audiences and find the threads of the tragic in Shylock's role very easy to grasp:

> *'Still have I borne it with a patient shrug,*
> *For sufferance is the badge of all our tribe.'*

There is no difficulty whatsoever in sympathising with Shylock's righteous indignation at the impertinence of being asked to bail out a bitter adversary who closes off every avenue of friendship.

> *'"Fair sir, you spat on me on Wednesday last;*
> *You spurn'd me such a day; another time*
> *You call'd me dog — and for these courtesies*
> *I'll lend you thus much moneys"?'*

Shylock's role is certainly a tragic one if he means it when he offers Antonio not only the money but friendship as well. But then that is the big question. What do you think?

Whatever our verdict to these questions, it is clear that the great dramatist has already transformed the stock Jewish villain into a deep and authentic character whose predicament is imaginatively grasped. Hypocritical, avaricious, spiteful he may be, but the author has endowed him with flesh and blood and, as he will remind us in time:

> *'If you prick us, do we not bleed?'* (3.1.59)

ANTONIO

Some Inconsistencies Come To Light

Antonio's character does not come unblemished from this scene. The man who tolerates a rogue's gallery of hangers-on in the first scene and who has been so generous to Bassanio has given Shylock nothing but a hard time:

> *'You call me misbeliever, cut-throat dog,*
> *And spit upon my Jewish gaberdine,*
> *... did void your rheum upon my beard,*
> *And foot me as you spurn a stranger cur*
> *Over your threshold.'*

Furthermore, Antonio does not propose to mend his ways:

> *'I am as like to call thee so again,*
> *To spit on thee again, to spurn thee too.'*

There is an extent to which Antonio can only blame himself for Shylock's recriprocal hatred.

Antonio is also inconsistent when it comes to principles. One of his principles is that he is totally opposed to usury.

> *'I do never use it.'*

Yet he will *'break a custom'* not on some life-or-death issue but because a friend wants to be fitted out in style to impress a lady! Taking *'interest'* is not acceptable to Antonio but *'venture'* is. What is sauce for the goose is not sauce for the gander.

Naivety Or Arrogance?

Antonio puts his life in the hands of the mortal enemy he has every reason to mistrust. Is it naivety, we wonder, or could it be that Antonio regards the danger to his person explicit in the bond as unworthy of consideration? Could it be that Antonio would expect to get away with it if the worst came to the worst? After all, Venice was a Christian society and Shylock was an outsider who might not find the Venetian legal system very sympathetic if it came to the crunch!

BASSANIO

Good-Hearted But Ineffectual

Bassanio left us with an unfavourable impression in Scene I and we watch him here to see if he redeems himself. The verdict is a mixed one: we observe a man who is well-meaning but who maintains that ineptitude which left him borrowing money in the first place.

Bassanio is clearly good-hearted. His gregarious and spontaneous nature is open even to Shylock:

> *'If it please you to dine with us.'*

His love and friendship for Antonio is also clearly genuine; he worries that he has got his friend into something sinister:

> *'You shall not seal to such a bond for me:*
> *I'll rather dwell in my necessity.'*

But Bassanio is also somewhat naive and ineffectual. He delivers Antonio into the hands of a known enemy, and, even though he suspects Shylock, he allows the arrangement to go ahead.

Act 2

Scene 1

*Belmont. A room in Portia's house. Enter the Prince of Morocco
and his followers; Portia, and Nerissa*

Morocco

Mislike[1] me not for my complexion,
The shadow'd livery[2] of the burnish'd[3] sun,
To whom I am a neighbour, and near bred.
Bring me the fairest creature northward born,
Where Phoebus'[4] fire scarce thaws the icicles,
And let us make incision[5] for your love,
To prove whose blood is reddest, his or mine,
I tell thee, lady, this aspect[6] of mine
Hath fear'd[7] the valiant: by my love, I swear
The best regarded virgins of our clime[8]   10
Have lov'd it too: I would not change this hue,[9]
Except to steal your thoughts, my gentle queen.

Portia

In terms of choice I am not solely led
By nice direction of a maiden's eyes;
Besides, the lottery of my destiny
Bars me the right of voluntary choosing:
But if my father had not scanted[10] me
And hedg'd[11] me by his wit, to yield myself
His wife who wins me by that means I told you,
Yourself, renowned prince, then stood as fair   20
As any comer I have look'd on yet
For my affection.

Morocco

      Even for that I thank you :
Therefore, I pray you, lead me to the caskets
To try my fortune. By this scimitar[12]—
That slew the Sophy[13],and a Persian prince
That won three fields of Sultan Solyman[14]—
I would o'erstare the sternest eyes that look;
Outbrave the heart most daring on the earth;
Pluck the young sucking cubs from the she-bear;
Yea, mock the lion when he roars for prey,   30
To win thee, lady. But, alas the while!
If Hercules[15] and Lichas[16] play at dice
Which is the better man, the greater throw

[1] dislike
[2] uniform
[3] bright

[4] sun-god
[5] cut in the skin

[6] appearance
[7] frightened
[8] climate or country
[9] colour

[10] restricted
[11] bound

[12] sword
[13] Shah of Persia
[14] Sultan of Turkey

[15] The Super-man of classical mythology
[16] Hercules' servant

[17]another name for Hercules

May turn by fortune from the weaker hand:
So is Alcides[17] beaten by his page;
And so may I, blind fortune leading me,
Miss that which one unworthier may attain,
And die with grieving.

Portia

      You must take your chance;
And either not attempt to choose at all,
Or swear before you choose, if you choose wrong,   *40*
Never to speak to lady afterward

[18]warned

In way of marriage: therefore be advis'd.[18]

Morocco

Nor will not: come, bring me unto my chance.

Portia

First, forward to the temple: after dinner

[19]gamble

Your hazard[19] shall be made.

Morocco

     Good fortune then!
To make me blest or cursed'st among men!

[Exeunt

Summary

The Prince of Morocco Woos Portia

At Belmont, the Prince of Morocco is making a case for himself. He asks Portia not to reject him on account of his black skin, for underneath it is the reddest blood and the bravest heart. Portia reminds him courteously that she has no choice in the matter and that he must take his chances like the others. He must also swear like every other suitor that if he chooses the wrong casket he will never marry. Morocco is apprehensive at the extent to which the outcome depends on chance and wants to get it over with immediately. Ceremony prevails, however, and he must wait until after dinner.

Scene Analysis

The tension and suspense of Act 1, Scene III is relieved by a scene full of visual and verbal pomp. The traditional stage direction is that Morocco and his followers, their black skins accentuated by their white moorish gowns, enter in regal procession to the flourish of coronets and mingle with the finely dressed ladies of Portia's household.

A Game Of Chance

Act 2, Scene I is the first episode in the casket story which fills the three months which must elapse before the bond story comes to a head.

The recurring theme of the scene is that of chance, of what Portia calls *'the lottery of my destiny'* or the *'blind fortune leading me'* which leaves the Prince of Morocco in such trepidation. It is a very different note to that on which the previous scene ended where Antonio expressed such unquestioning confidence in the future.

Chance is always attended by the danger of failure and if Portia's prospective suitors *'choose wrong'* they are bound:

> *'Never to speak to lady afterward*
> *In way of marriage:'*

The intimidating conditions of the casket game have caused many suitors to return home without taking the risk. It is no wonder that Morocco ponders anxiously that he may:

> *'Miss that which one unworthier may attain,*
> *And die with grieving.'*

Mislike me not for my complexion,
The shadow'd livery of the burnish'd sun: (Prince of Morocco, Act 2, Sc I)

Characters

THE PRINCE OF MOROCCO

A Winning Hesitancy!

For one whose appearance is so imposing, Morocco begins and ends the scene with a surprising degree of self-effacement and circumspection. His opening words are defensive:

> *'Mislike me not for my complexion,'*

His closing utterances are equally apprehensive and anxious:

> *'Good fortune then!*
> *To make me blest or cursed'st among men!'*

Like Shylock, Morocco is an alien figure in the play who feels it necessary in some way to apologise for being different. But whereas Shylock felt it necessary to tell people he had blood in his veins at all, it is sufficient for Morocco to explain that his blood is as red as anyone else's. To the Elizabethans red blood was a sign of spirit and courage.

For all his hesitancy and circumspection, Morocco still manages to speak of himself in superlatives. His language is rich and rhetorical and full of poetry and it reveals the pride and self-esteem of a man who knows he is respected and sought after in his own world.

> *'I tell thee, lady, this aspect of mine*
> *Hath fear'd the valiant: by my love, I swear*
> *The best regarded virgins of our clime*
> *Have lov'd it too:'*

Morocco would not want to change a thing about himself unless it were to win him the affections of Portia. He would do anything, in fact, to win Portia:

> *'I would o'erstare the sternest eyes that look;*
> *Outbrave the heart most daring on the earth;*
> *Pluck the young sucking cubs from the she-bear;*
> *Yea, mock the lion when he roars for prey,*
> *To win thee, lady.'*

Another Look At Portia

In this scene, we meet Portia for the second time and we find that the young woman who was girlish in the intimacy of Nerissa's company here assumes the lady-like qualities of the courteous hostess who is tactful and humorous and graceful under pressure.

Portia faces with equanimity the prospect of having as her husband a man who, however impressive, is not of her own choosing. Though it continues to rankle, she never flinches for a moment from the terms of her father's will:

'...the lottery of my destiny
Bars me the right of voluntary choosing:'

Though 'scanted' and 'hedg'd' by her father's 'wit', Portia is still capable of humour. To tell Morocco that he:

'...stood as fair
As any comer I have look'd on yet...'

at once puns on the colour of his skin which is anything but 'fair' and shares with the audience the unspoken sentiment that the standard has not been very high after all.

Portia is unruffled by Morocco's anxiety to get things over with. She is the hostess and business, however compelling, must wait until she has dined with her guest.

Scene II

Venice. The street outside Shylock's house.
Enter Launcelot Gobbo

Launcelot

Certainly my conscience will serve[1] me to run from
this Jew my master. The fiend[2] is at mine elbow, and
tempts me, saying to me, 'Gobbo, Launcelot Gobbo,
good Launcelot,' or 'good Gobbo,' or 'good Launcelot
Gobbo, use your legs, take the start, run away.' My
conscience says, 'No; take heed, honest Launcelot;
take heed, honest Gobbo;' or, as aforesaid, 'honest
Launcelot Gobbo; do not run; scorn running with thy
heels.' Well, the most courageous fiend bids me
pack:[3] '*Via!*'[4] says the fiend; 'away!' says the   10
fiend; 'for the heavens, rouse up a brave mind,'
says the fiend, 'and run.' Well, my conscience,
hanging about the neck of my heart, says very wisely
to me, 'My honest friend Launcelot, being an honest
man's son,' — or rather an honest woman's son, for,
indeed, my father did something smack,[5] something
grow to,[6] he had a kind of taste — well, my conscience
says, 'Launcelot, budge[7] not.' 'Budge!' says the
fiend. 'Budge not!' says my conscience.
'Conscience,' say I, 'you counsel well;' 'Fiend,'   20
say I, 'you counsel well.' to be ruled by my
conscience, I should stay with the Jew my master,
who (God bless the mark!) is a kind of devil; and, to
run away from the Jew, I should be ruled by the
fiend, who (saving your reverence) is the devil
himself. Certainly, the Jew is the very devil
incarnation;[8] and, in my conscience, my conscience is

[1] assist
[2] devil

[3] be off
[4] away

[5] dishonourable
[6] unpleasant

[7] move

[8] he means 'incarnate', i.e. in the flesh

but a kind of hard conscience, to offer to counsel
me to stay with the Jew. The fiend gives the more   30
friendly counsel: I will run, fiend; my heels are
at your commandment; I will run.

Enter Old Gobbo, with a basket

Gobbo

Master young man, you; I pray you, which is the way
to Master Jew's?

Launcelot

[Aside] O heavens! this is my true-begotten father,
who, being more than sand-blind,[9] high gravel-blind,[10]
knows me not: I will try confusions with him.

Gobbo

Master young gentleman, I pray you, which is the way
to Master Jew's?

Launcelot

Turn up on your right hand at the next turning, but,   40
at the next turning of all, on your left; marry,[11]
at the very next turning, turn of no hand, but turn
down indirectly to the Jew's house.

Gobbo

By God's sonties,[12] 'twill be a hard way to hit. Can you
tell me whether one Launcelot, that dwells with him,
dwell with him or no?

Launcelot

Talk you of young Master Launcelot? [Aside] Mark
me now; now will I raise the waters,[13] Talk you of
young Master Launcelot?

Gobbo

No 'master', sir, but a poor man's son; his father,
though I say 't, is an honest, exceeding poor man,   50
and, God be thanked, well to live.

Launcelot

Well, let his father be what 'a[14] will, we talk of
young Master Launcelot.

Gobbo

Your worship's friend, and Launcelot, sir.

Launcelot

But pray you, *ergo*[15] old man, *ergo*, I beseech you,
talk you of young Master Launcelot?

---

[9]half-blind
[10]almost totally blind

[11]by the Virgin Mary

[12]saints

[13]bring tears to his eyes

[14]he

[15]Latin for 'therefore'

Gobbo

Of Launcelot, an't please your mastership.

Launcelot

Ergo, Master Launcelot. Talk not of Master
Launcelot, father; for the young gentleman
(according to fates and destinies and such odd   *60*
sayings, the sisters three[16] and such branches of
learning) is, indeed, deceased; or, as you would say
in plain terms, gone to heaven.

[16]the Fates in classical
mythology who controlled
human destiny

Gobbo

Marry, God forbid! the boy was the very staff of my
age, my very prop.

Launcelot

[Aside] Do I look like a cudgel or a hovel-post,[17]
a staff or a prop? Do you know me, father?

[17]a timber post supporting
the roof of a shack

Gobbo

Alack the day! I know you not, young gentleman: but I
pray you, tell me, is my boy — God rest his soul! —
alive or dead?   *70*

Launcelot

Do you not know me, father?

Gobbo

Alack, sir, I am sand-blind; I know you not.

Launcelot

Nay, indeed, if you had your eyes, you might fail of the
knowing me: it is a wise father that knows his
own child. Well, old man, I will tell you news of
your son. *[Kneels]* Give me your blessing: truth will come
to light; murder cannot be hid long; a man's son
may, but, in the end, truth will out.

Gobbo

Pray you, sir, stand up. I am sure you are not
Launcelot, my boy.   *80*

Launcelot

Pray you, let's have no more fooling about it, but
give me your blessing: I am Launcelot, your boy
that was, your son that is, your child that shall
be.

Gobbo

I cannot think you are my son.

Launcelot

I know not what I shall think of that; but I am

Launcelot, the Jew's man, and I am sure Margery your
wife is my mother.

Gobbo

Her name is Margery, indeed: I'll be sworn, if thou
be Launcelot, thou art mine own flesh and blood.   90
Lord worshipped might he be! what a beard hast thou
got! thou hast got more hair on thy chin than
Dobbin my fill-horse[18] has on his tail.

18cart-horse

Launcelot

It should seem then that Dobbin's tail grows
backward: I am sure he had more hair of his tail
than I have of my face, when I last saw him.

Gobbo

Lord, how art thou changed! How dost thou and thy
master agree? I have brought him a present. How
'gree[19] you now?

19agree

Launcelot

Well, well: but, for mine own part, as I have set   100
up my rest to run away, so I will not rest till I
have run some ground. My master's a very Jew: give
him a present? give him a halter! I am famished in
his service; you may tell every finger I have with
my ribs. Father, I am glad you are come: give me
your present to one Master Bassanio, who, indeed,
gives rare new liveries.[20] If I serve not him, I
will run as far as God has any ground. O rare
fortune! here comes the man: to him, father; for I
am a Jew, if I serve the Jew any longer.   110

20uniforms, jobs

Enter Bassanio with Leonardo and other Servants

Bassanio

You may do so; but let it be so hasted that supper be
ready at the farthest by five of the clock. See
these letters delivered; put the liveries to making;
and desire Gratiano to come anon[21] to my lodging.

21at once

[Exit a Servant

Launcelot

To him, father.

Gobbo

God bless your worship!

Bassanio

Gramercy![22] wouldst thou aught with me?

22many thanks

Gobbo

Here's my son, sir, a poor boy—

Launcelot

Not a poor boy, sir, but the rich Jew's man; that
would, sir — as my father shall specify—   *120*

Gobbo

He hath a great infection,[23] sir (as one would say)   [23]he means 'affection'
to serve—

Launcelot

Indeed, the short and the long is, I serve the Jew, and
have a desire, as my father shall specify—

Gobbo

His master and he (saving your worship's reverence)
are scarce cater-cousins.[24]   [24]great friends

Launcelot

To be brief, the very truth is that the Jew having done
me wrong, doth cause me—as my father, being, I
hope, an old man, shall frutify[25] unto you—   [25]he means 'fructify' or to notify

Gobbo

I have here a dish of doves that I would bestow upon   *130*
your worship, and my suit[26] is—   [26]request

Launcelot

In very brief, the suit is impertinent[27] to myself, as   [27]he means 'pertinent', i.e. relevant
your worship shall know by this honest old man; and,
though I say it, though old man, yet (poor man) my father.

Bassanio

One speak for both. What would you?

Launcelot

Serve you, sir.

Gobbo

That is the very defect[28] of the matter, sir.   [28]he means 'effect', i.e. conclusion

Bassanio

I know thee well; thou hast obtain'd thy suit:
Shylock thy master spoke with me this day,
And hath preferr'd[29] thee, if it be preferment[30]   *140*   [29]recommended
To leave a rich Jew's service, to become   [30]promotion
The follower of so poor a gentleman.

Launcelot

The old proverb is very well parted[31] between my   [31]divided
master Shylock and you, sir: you have 'the grace of
God', sir, and he hath 'enough'.

Bassanio

Thou speak'st it well. Go, father, with thy son.
Take leave of thy old master, and inquire
My lodging out. *[To his Servants]* Give him a livery
More guarded[32] than his fellows': see it done.

Launcelot

Father, in. I cannot get a service, no! I have   150
ne'er a tongue in my head. Well, *[Looking at his hand]* if any
in Italy have a fairer table[33] which doth offer to
swear upon a book, I shall have good fortune. Go to;
here's a simple line of life: here's a small trifle
of wives: alas! fifteen wives is nothing: eleven
widows and nine maids is a simple coming-in[34] for one
man; and the to 'scape[35] drowning thrice, and to be
in peril of my life with the edge of a feather-bed;
here are simple 'scapes. Well, if Fortune be a
woman, she's a good wench for this gear.[36] Father,
come; I'll take my leave of the Jew in the twinkling of an eye.*160*

[Exeunt Launcelot and Old Gobbo

Bassanio

I pray thee, good Leonardo, think on this.
These things being bought, and orderly bestow'd,[37]
Return in haste, for I do feast tonight
My best-esteem'd acquaintance. Hie thee, go.

help prepare for a meal tonight

Leonardo

My best endeavours shall be done herein.

Enter Gratiano

Gratiano

Where's your master?

Leonardo

Yonder, sir, he walks.   *over there*

[Exit

Gratiano

Signior Bassanio!

Bassanio

Gratiano!

Gratiano

I have a suit to you.   *I have a question*

32 with more braid on it

33 palm

34 income
35 escape

36 business

37 put away

Bassanio

You have obtain'd it.   *I'll help*   170

Gratiano

You must not deny me: I must go with you to Belmont.

Bassanio

Why, then you must. But hear thee, Gratiano;
Thou art too wild, too rude, and bold of voice;   *You need to behave*
Parts[38] that become thee[39] happily enough,   [38]qualities
And in such eyes as ours appear not faults—   [39]suit you
But where thou art not known, why, there they show
Something too liberal.[40] Pray thee, take pain   [40]free and easy
To allay[41] with some cold drops of modesty   [41]moderate
Thy skipping spirit, lest, through thy wild behaviour,
I be misconster'd[42] in the place I go to,   180   [42]misunderstood
And lose my hopes.

Gratiano

    Signior Bassanio, hear me:
If I do not put on a sober habit,[43]   [43]dress and behaviour
Talk with respect, and swear but now and then,   *I will be*
Wear prayer-books in my pocket, look demurely,[44]   *really*   [44]gravely
Nay more, while grace is saying, hood[45] mine eyes   *good*   [45]cover
Thus with my hat, and sigh, and say 'amen',
Use all the observance of civility,[46]   [46]civilised behaviour
Like one well studied in a sad ostent[47]   [47]appearance
To please his grandam, never trust me more.

Bassanio

Well, we shall see your bearing.[48]   *We'll see*   190   [48]how you behave yourself

Gratiano

Nay, but I bar[49] tonight; you shall not gauge[50] me   [49]make an exception of
By what we do tonight.   [50]judge

Bassanio

    No, that were pity:
I would entreat you rather to put on
Your boldest suit of mirth, for we have friends   *Fine*
That purpose[51] merriment. But fare you well: [51]are planning
I have some business.

Gratiano

And I must to Lorenzo and the rest;
But we will visit you at supper-time.

                                        [Exeunt

Summary

A Clown For Hire

On a street outside Shylock's house Launcelot Gobbo, Shylock's servant, is fiercely debating with himself whether or not he should run away from his master. As he resolves to go, Old Gobbo, his father, whom he has not seen for years, enters looking for his son. His eyesight is so poor that he does not recognise Launcelot who plays the cruel trick on him of reporting that his son is dead. Having fooled the old man and enjoyed the trick, Launcelot reveals himself and engages his father's help in seeking employment from Bassanio who enters shortly afterwards. Bassanio agrees to take on Launcelot and sends him to his house to be suitably dressed for his new position.

Gratiano now enters and he too seeks a favour from Bassanio. He wishes to accompany Bassanio to Belmont. Bassanio grants his wish but insists that Gratiano be on his best behaviour.

Scene Analysis

From The Sublime To The Ridiculous

The noble rhetoric of the Prince of Morocco gives way to the preposterous antics of Launcelot Gobbo. Shakespeare indulges his audience's appetite for slapstick and gives scope to the clowning talents of his company. There is much verbal humour also. We are assailed with a barrage of tongue-twisters, malapropisms, confusions, mispronounced words and inverted proverbs:

> '...it is a wise father that knows his own child.'

Without the slapstick, however, the verbal humour is somewhat flat: nowhere more than here do we experience the inadequacy of drama reduced to words upon a page.

Developments In The Plot

Scene II is a minor scene but it does present us with two details central to the plot's development. It sees the promotion of Launcelot to Bassanio's service which in turn helps to develop the relationship between Lorenzo and Jessica.

Characters

LAUNCELOT

The Clown

Launcelot Gobbo, as the name suggests, is the clown figure of the play. He prances about the stage in antics that are rich in gesture and facial expression. He mimics both his conscience and the devil who sandwich him in a mock-heroic duel about whether or not he should run away from his master.

> '"Budge!" says the fiend. "Budge not!" says my conscience.'

A Misplaced Love For Fine Words

Launcelot has a fatal fascination for fine-sounding words which he does not understand. He constantly overextends his vocabulary. Shylock, he thinks: *'is the very devil incarnation'* which is why he approaches Bassanio with a suit *'impertinent'* to himself. Bassanio recognises that Launcelot's talents are those of the jester and that he should be decked out accordingly with additional decoration on his uniform:

> *'Give him a livery*
> *More guarded than his fellows:'*

Launcelot's More Serious Dramatic Purpose

(a) By leaving Shylock's service and going to work for Bassanio, Launcelot becomes a go-between for Lorenzo and Jessica and consequently a key figure in their elopement.

(b) Launcelot also tells us what it is like to live with and work for Shylock. Shylock, he tells us, *'is the very devil'* whose miserliness has left its imprint on Launcelot's figure if not his sense of humour:

> *'I am famished in his service; you may tell every finger I have with my ribs.'*

OLD GOBBO

Like Son, Like Father

Old Gobbo shares his son's fatal attraction for words that are beyond him. He says *'infection'* for *'affection'* and *'defect'* for *'effect'*. He is a rustic man whose simplicity is accentuated by blindness. His main function is to be the butt of Launcelot's practical jokes and confusions.

BASSANIO

A More Favourable Impression

Bassanio comes on stage full of the energy and generosity with which he approaches life. He is spending his borrowed money liberally and is arranging a feast at which he wants everyone to be happy.

> *'I would entreat you rather to put on*
> *Your boldest suit of mirth...'*

He is also creating employment and one of the *'rare new liveries'* goes to Launcelot after the shortest of interviews and the most dubious of references.

'Shylock thy master spoke with me this day,
And hath preferr'd thee,'

Bassanio is obliging also to Gratiano whose request he grants in the most impulsive manner.

Gratiano: *'I have a suit to you'*

Bassanio: *'You have obtain'd it'*

This spontaneous generosity contrasts sharply with the calculating miserliness of Shylock as reported by Launcelot. Shylock may be rich, Launcelot tells us, but Bassanio has *'the grace of God'*.

GRATIANO

A Problem For Bassanio

The problem with Gratiano as Bassanio sees it, is that he is such a loquacious and high-spirited extrovert that he may give the wrong impression in Belmont.

'Thou art too wild, too rude, and bold of voice;'

Bassanio feels it necessary to ask Gratiano *'To ally with some cold drops of modesty'* his *'skipping spirit'* and his *'wild behaviour'*.

Gratiano undertakes not to let Bassanio down and to pretend to be other than he is. He will *'put on a sober habit'* and:

'Use all the observance of civility,
Like one well studied in a sad ostent...'

He will be good, but not quite yet:

'...you shall not gauge me
By what we do tonight.'

Scene III

Venice. The street outside Shylock's house.
Enter Jessica and Launcelot

Jessica

I am sorry thou wilt leave my father so:
Our house is hell, and thou, a merry devil,
Didst rob it of some taste of tediousness.
But fare thee well; there is a ducat for thee—
And, Launcelot, soon at supper shalt thou see
Lorenzo, who is thy new master's guest:

she is sorry
he is leaving.

Give him this letter — do it secretly.
And so farewell: I would not have my father
See me in talk with thee.

Launcelot

Adieu! tears exhibit[1] my tongue. Most beautiful
pagan, most sweet Jew! If a Christian do not play the
knave and get thee, I am much deceived. But, adieu!
these foolish drops do something drown my manly
spirit: adieu!

he's crying   10

[1] he means, 'inhibit' or restrain

Jessica

Farewell, good Launcelot.   [Exit Launcelot
Alack, what heinous[2] sin is it in me
To be asham'd to be my father's child!
But though I am a daughter to his blood,
I am not to his manners. O Lorenzo,
If thou keep promise, I shall end this strife,
Become a Christian, and thy loving wife.

she's ashamed of her father but she's different to him.

[2] hateful

20

[Exit

Summary

Launcelot's Farewell To Jessica

On the street outside Shylock's house, Launcelot is saying farewell to Shylock's daughter, Jessica. She is sorry to see him go as she will miss his cheerful company from what was otherwise a very unhappy home. She gives Launcelot a coin and a letter to be delivered secretly to Lorenzo who is to be a guest of Bassanio that evening. She is anxious not to be seen by her father.

Launcelot is overcome with emotion and unable to say very much other than farewell.

Left alone, Jessica confesses somewhat guiltily that she is ashamed of her father. Though she has his blood she is glad that she inherits none of his characteristics. She plans to end her misery by eloping with Lorenzo and becoming a Christian.

Scene Analysis

Scene III is one of the multiplicity of short scenes in Act 2 which give the impression of time passing. Short though it be, the scene fulfils a number of important functions:

1. We are **introduced to Shylock's daughter Jessica** whose romantic love affair with Lorenzo parallels and contrasts with the more central love story of Bassanio and Portia.

2. The **play gathers pace** as Jessica informs us of her plans to elope with Lorenzo.

> '...O Lorenzo,
> If thou keep promise, I shall end this strife,
> Become a Christian, and thy loving wife.'

3. The **conspiracy against Shylock deepens** and Jessica is up to her neck in it.

> '... do it secretly.
> ... I would not have my father
> See me in talk with thee.'

Having lost a servant, Shylock is about to suffer a more grievous loss. Total isolation hangs over him as the Christians, so often his victors in the past, are about to steal his daughter.

> I am sorry thou wilt leave my father so:
> Our house is hell, and thou, a merry devil,
> Didst rob it of some taste of tediousness.   (Jessica, Act 2, Sc III)

The Atmosphere Of The Scene

The street outside Shylock's house is an uneasy place where people look over their shoulders. The talk is of robbery, secrecy and deception, of knaves, and of sin, shame and strife.

Characters

JESSICA

Jessica is a very insecure young lady who finds very little to cherish in her circumstances. Motherless in a house that is a hell, she is driven into secrecy and rebellion by a tyrannical father of whom she is acutely ashamed.

Jessica is uncomfortable even in her attitude towards her father:

> *'Alack, what heinous sin is it in me*
> *To be asham'd to be my father's child!'*

Her only consolation has been the way Launcelot used to cheer her bleak world.

> *'...thou, a merry devil,*
> *Didst rob it of some taste of tediousness.'*

It is no wonder that she is sorry to see Launcelot go.

The scene ends for her on a continuing note of insecurity for Lorenzo has to *'keep promise'* if she is to *'end this strife'*.

LAUNCELOT

For all his verbosity in the previous scene, Launcelot has few words here. The *'merry devil'* who robbed Shylock's house of its *'taste of tediousness'* is reduced to tears and inarticulateness at the prospect of leaving Jessica.

SHYLOCK

Though absent from the scene, Shylock is portrayed as a villain whose daughter is ashamed of him and whose house is a tedious hell mitigated only by the cheering presence of a merry servant.

Scene IV

Venice. The street outside Shylock's house.
Enter Gratiano, Lorenzo, Salerio, and Solanio

Lorenzo

Nay, we will slink away in supper-time,
Disguise us at my lodging, and return
All in an hour.

Gratiano

We have not made good preparation.

Salerio

We have not spoke us yet of torch-bearers.

Solanio

¹artisitically arranged

'Tis vile unless it may be quaintly order'd¹
And better, in my mind, not undertook.

Lorenzo

²to get ready

'Tis now but four o'clock: we have two hours
To furnish us.²

Enter Launcelot, with a letter

Friend Launcelot, what's the news?

Launcelot

³open
⁴inform you

And it shall please you to break up³ this, it   10
shall seem to signify.⁴

Lorenzo

I know the hand: in faith, 'tis a fair hand;
And whiter than the paper it writ on
Is the fair hand that writ.

Gratiano

Love news, in faith.

Launcelot

By your leave, sir.

Lorenzo

Whither goest thou?

Launcelot

Marry, sir, to bid my old master, the Jew, to sup
tonight with my new master, the Christian.

Lorenzo

Hold here, take this: tell gentle Jessica
I will not fail her; speak it privately.   20
Go, gentlemen,   *[Exit Launcelot*

Will you prepare you for this masque tonight?
I am provided of a torch-bearer.

Salerio

Ay, marry, I'll be gone about it straight.

Solanio

And so will I.

Lorenzo

Meet me and Gratiano
At Gratiano's lodging some hour hence.

Salerio

'Tis good we do so.

[*Exeunt Salerio and Solanio*

Gratiano

Was not that letter from fair Jessica?

Lorenzo

I must needs tell thee all. She hath directed[5]   [5]instructed
How I shall take her from her father's house;   *30*
What gold and jewels she is furnish'd[6] with;   [6]supplied
What page's suit she hath in readiness.
If e'er the Jew her father come to heaven,
It will be for his gentle daughter's sake;
And never dare misfortune cross her foot,
Unless she do it under this excuse,
That she is issue to[7] a faithless Jew.   [7]a child of
Come, go with me: peruse[8] this as thou goest.   [8]examine
Fair Jessica shall be my torch-bearer.   [*Exeunt*

Summary

A Masquerade Is Planned

Bassanio's friends are planning something special for Bassanio's going-away dinner that evening. Lorenzo is at the centre of preparations and Gratiano, Salerio and Solanio are anxious that everything be done properly, even to the extent of hiring torch-bearers.

Launcelot enters on his way to invite Shylock to the party and delivers the letter from Jessica to Lorenzo. Lorenzo sends Jessica a reply through Launcelot that he will not let her down. He now seems satisfied that he has a torch-bearer!

When Salerio and Solanio leave, Lorenzo confides in Gratiano the contents of the letter. Jessica plans to disguise herself as a page on that very night and to elope with Lorenzo. And she is not coming empty-handed: she will have stolen a substantial dowry in gold and jewels from her father. It is clear now that Jessica will be Lorenzo's torch-bearer.

Scene Analysis

Scene IV is filled with fragmentary conversation and all-round bustle and gives the **impression of many things about to happen**. Plans for the elopement unfold and it becomes clear that Shylock is not only going to lose his daughter but *'What gold and jewels she is furnish'd with;'* as well.

A Masque

The action centres on the masque which Lorenzo is planning as a surprise-ending to Bassanio's party. Traditionally a masque or masquerade comprised a group elaborately disguised in fancy dress and masks who paraded through the streets and made a formal entry to a social gathering accompanied by music and torch-bearers. It generally occurred after supper and surprised guests and hosts alike. After their ceremonial entry, the masquers usually joined the other guests in a dance.

Shylock is being invited to something very different from what he expects and something of which he would disapprove very strongly. The vivacity and enthusiasm going on in the street outside his house would certainly not be entertained inside.

Neither the masque nor the supper ever happens, however. Perhaps Shakespeare thought that there wasn't enough time for it or perhaps he decided to spare Shylock being affronted by Jessica in a page's outfit lest our sympathy for him would get out of hand.

Characters

This short scene gives us but fragmentary snippets of the characters involved, who do little more than remain themselves. For instance Salerio and Solanio remain as socially polished and otherwise bland as ever. They are shallow characters for whom appearances matter most:

> 'Tis vile unless it may be quaintly order'd...'

Strangely enough, the one character developed significantly is not present in the scene at all. It is **Jessica**. If Lorenzo seems to be so central to the action, it is equally clear that Jessica is laying down the law.

> 'She hath directed
> How I shall take her from her father's house;'

And, while Lorenzo refers to her as 'gentle Jessica', it appears that she is quite capable of looking after her own interests as is evidenced by:

> 'What gold and jewels she is furnish'd with;'

She is patently devoid of sympathy for her avaricious father Shylock and the only thanks she offers for her austere upbringing is to rob him of as much as she can.

Scene V

Venice. The street outside Shylock's house.
Enter Shylock, and Launcelot

Shylock

Well, thou shalt see, thy eyes shall be thy judge
The difference of[1] old Shylock and Bassanio—
What, Jessica! — thou shalt not gormandize[2]
As thou hast done with me — What, Jessica!—
And sleep and snore, and rend apparel out[3]—
Why, Jessica, I say!

I'm a better boss

Calling to Jessica

[1] between
[2] over-eat

[3] wear out clothes

Launcelot

      Why, Jessica!

Shylock

Who bids thee call? I do not bid thee call.

Launcelot

Your worship was wont[4] to tell me that
I could do nothing without bidding.

You said I didn't do anything without being told.

[4] accustomed

Enter Jessica

Jessica

Call you? What is your will?   10

Shylock

I am bid forth[5] to supper, Jessica;
There are my keys. But wherefore should I go?
I am not bid for love: they flatter me.
But yet I'll go in hate, to feed upon
The prodigal[6] Christian. Jessica, my girl,
Look to my house. I am right loath to go:
There is some ill a-brewing towards my rest,
For I did dream of money-bags tonight.

They are trying to keep him sweet

Going to lose money

[5] invited out

[6] wasteful

Launcelot

I beseech you, sir, go: my young master doth expect
your reproach.[7]   *Go on they're waiting*   20

[7] he means 'approach'

Shylock

So do I his.

Launcelot

And they have conspired together: I will not say you
shall see a masque; but if you do, then it was not
for nothing that my nose fell a-bleeding on
Black Monday[8] last, at six o'clock i' the morning,
falling out that year on Ash Wednesday was four
year in th' afternoon.

Talking Nonsense

[8] Easter Monday

Shylock

What, are there masques? Hear you me, Jessica:
Lock up my doors, and when you hear the drum
⁹flute with a twisted neck
¹⁰windows
And the vile squealing of the wry-neck'd fife⁹,   30
Clamber not you up to the casements¹⁰ then,
Nor thrust your head into the public street
To gaze on Christian fools with varnish'd faces,
But stop my house's ears —I mean my casements—
¹¹empty foolishness
Let not the sound of shallow foppery¹¹ enter
My sober house. By Jacob's staff I swear
I have no mind of feasting forth tonight;
But I will go. Go you before me, sirrah;
Say I will come.

Look up the house.

Launcelot

I will go before, sir. Mistress, look out at window,   40
for all this:
      There will come a Christian by,   *Lorenzo*
      Will be worth a Jewess' eye.

                                       [Exit Launcelot

Shylock

¹²a Gentile
What says that fool of Hagar's¹² offspring, ha?

Jessica

His words were, 'Farewell, mistress'; nothing else.

Shylock

¹³fool
The patch¹³ is kind enough, but a huge feeder;
Snail-slow in profit, and he sleeps by day
¹⁴bees who do not work
More than the wild cat: drones¹⁴ hive not with me;
Therefore I part with him, and part with him
To one that I would have him help to waste
His borrow'd purse. Well, Jessica, go in—   50
Perhaps I will return immediately—
Do as I bid you; shut doors after you:
¹⁵If you take care of what
you have you will prosper
'Fast bind, fast find',¹⁵
A proverb never stale in thrifty mind.   *[Exit*

He is glad to be rid of Lancelot.

Jessica

¹⁶thwarted
Farewell; and if my fortune be not cross'd,¹⁶
I have a father, you a daughter, lost.   *[Exit*

Summary

Anxious Moments

Launcelot has come to Shylock's house to deliver Lorenzo's reply to Jessica. He has bumped into Shylock who tells him that he will not have it quite so easy under Bassanio as he allegedly has had it under his former master!

Shylock interrupts his conversation with Launcelot to call repeatedly for Jessica: he is going out to Bassanio's dinner party and is leaving her in charge. He is going reluctantly; he does not think that the invitation is sincere and he has had a premonition that some evil plot is being hatched against him.

Launcelot lets it slip that a masque is being planned and this increases Shylock's anxiety and launches him into an attack on the kind of cheap frivolity from which he wishes to protect both his house and his daughter.

Launcelot tells Jessica to be on the lookout for Lorenzo, and Jessica has to convince Shylock that Launcelot was merely saying goodbye.

Shylock admits that Launcelot is not a bad sort but he has found him too voracious in appetite and too easy-going to be profitable. He is only too happy at the prospect of Bassanio's resources being drained by Launcelot.

Despite his misgivings, Shylock finally sets out for Bassanio's house and leaves Jessica alone on the stage to foretell that before long, and if all goes well, he will have lost a daughter and she a father.

Scene Analysis

Dramatic Irony

Dramatic irony occurs when an audience is allowed to gather from a scene an idea or a message that runs contrary to what is happening or what is being said. The audience has information of which the character on the stage is unaware and in the light of which his utterances or actions appear as comic or tragic or downright pathetic.

The dramatic irony in this scene lies in the comic fact that a man who is obsessed with locking and guarding his possessions should leave in charge of them the very person who is in the process of robbing him.

> 'There are my keys …'
> 'Hear you me, Jessica:
> Lock up my doors…'

A further irony is that Shylock is also about to be robbed of his daughter while it is his material possessions that he is so concerned about.

Suspense

Launcelot and Jessica are anxious to get Shylock out of the way so that the elopement can take place. Shylock's indecision – *'But wherefore should I go?'* – is therefore tantalizing and tension is maintained by the danger that perhaps he *'will return immediately'*.

There is also a very real possibility that at any moment Launcelot will give the game away.

*Let not the sound of shallow foppery enter
My sober house.*   (Shylock, Act 2, Sc V)

Characters

SHYLOCK

A Second Appearance

Even in his absence, Shylock has been the dominant presence in the play since his first appearance in Act 1, Scene III. Much of the action has taken place outside his house and we have heard a lot about him. He now appears in person for only the second time in the play. Having met the public man in Act 1, Scene III, we now meet him at home.

Shylock At Home: A Miser And A 'Killjoy'

We have already had an unflattering picture of Shylock at home from both Jessica and Launcelot, and Shylock in person lives up to his reputation. He is a miser with a fixation on locking up his possessions, a man who dreams of *'money bags'* and starves his servant while thinking himself over-generous. Shylock's motto is:

> *'"Fast bind, fast find"*
> *A proverb never stale in thrifty mind.'*

Shylock despises warmth and festivity. He has *'no mind for feasting'* and he hates music:

> *'...when you hear the drum*
> *And the vile squealing of the wry-neck'd fife,*
> *Clamber not you up to the casements then...'*

Shylock would like to lock the world outside his casements as he locks his valuables inside.

> *'But stop my house's ears...*
> *Let not the sound of shallow foppery enter*
> *My sober house.'*

An Alien figure

The tide of sympathy flows against Shylock in this scene. The miserly killjoy in him elicits scorn and ridicule rather than sympathy and an audience can only smile when he leaves in charge of his house the very person who is robbing him. It is much easier to identify with the gaiety and liveliness of the young Venetians who are planning the evening's entertainment. Shylock is out of place amidst the festivity and colour of Venice: he is mean and calculating in a world which, if somewhat wayward, is impulsively generous and vivacious.

A Victim Also

But it is easy for the Venetians to be carefree and open: they are sure of their place in the sun. Shylock, on the other hand, is a member of a persecuted race who has had good reason in the past — as he has now — to be alert and suspicious.

> *'There is some ill a-brewing towards my rest.'*

Shylock has received no love from the society in which he lives and that lack of love has driven him to hate.

> *'I am not bid for love: they flatter me.*
> *But yet I'll go in hate...'*

Alone against the world, he relies on his only daughter.

> '... Jessica, my girl,
> Look to my house.'

But the one person Shylock feels he can rely on has duplicity on her lips and treachery in her heart. Shylock can depend on no one.

LAUNCELOT

Letting The Cat Out Of The Bag

As far as Shylock is concerned, Launcelot is a total waster:

> '... a huge feeder;
> Snail-slow in profit. ... (who) ... sleeps by day
> More than the wild cat:'

Even Shylock can admit, however, that there is no harm in the clown:

> 'The patch is kind enough'.

Launcelot's big mouth would be a burden to any conspiracy, however, and the *'merry devil'* threatens to *'rob'* the place of its *'taste of tediousness'* by informing Shylock of the coming masque and elopement.

> 'There will come a Christian by,
> Will be worth a Jewess' eye'.

The situation is barely saved by a combination of Jessica's track-covering and Shylock's bad hearing and perhaps by the fact that Launcelot is such a fool and speaks so much nonsense that no one will ever take him seriously anyway.

JESSICA

A Difficult Moment

Jessica is reluctant to answer Shylock's call because she is afraid to get involved in a conversation with both Launcelot and Shylock. Her worst fears are justified and she has to cover Launcelot's tracks with lies:

> 'His words were, "Farewell, mistress"; nothing else.'

She has lost all feeling for her father and her home:

> 'Farewell; and if my fortune be not cross'd,
> I have a father, you a daughter, lost.'

Scene VI

Venice. The street outside Shylock's house
Enter Gratiano and Salerio dressed as masquers

Gratiano

This is the penthouse[1] under which Lorenzo
Desir'd us to make stand.[2]

Salerio

      His hour is almost past.

Lorenzo is late

Gratiano

And it is marvel he out-dwells[3] his hour,
For lovers ever run before the clock.

Salerio

O ten times faster Venus' pigeons[4] fly
To seal love's bonds new-made, then they are wont
To keep obliged faith[5] unforfeited!

Gratiano

That ever holds:[6] who riseth from a feast
With that keen appetite that he sits down?
Where is the horse that doth untread[7] again   10
His tedious measures[8] with the unbated[9] fire
That he did pace them first? All things that are,
Are with more spirit chased than enjoy'd.
How like a younger[10] or a prodigal
The scarfed bark[11] puts from her native bay,
Hugg'd and embraced by the strumpet[12] wind!
How like the prodigal doth she return,
With over-weather'd ribs and ragged sails,
Lean, rent,[13] and beggar'd by the strumpet wind!

Enter Lorenzo

Salerio

Here comes Lorenzo: more of this hereafter.   20

Lorenzo

Sweet friends, your patience for my long abode;[14]
Not I but my affairs have made you wait:
When you shall please to play the thieves for wives,
I'll watch as long for you then. Approach;
Here dwells my father Jew. Ho! who's within?

Enter Jessica on the balcony, dressed as a boy

[1] a part of a house which projects out over a pavement
[2] wait

[3] out-stays

[4] the classical goddess of love had her chariot drawn by doves
[5] marriage vows

[6] is always true

[7] retrace
[8] steps
[9] undiminished

[10] younger son
[11] decorated ship
[12] unfaithful

[13] torn

[14] delay

Jessica

Who are you? Tell me, for more certainty,
Albeit I'll swear that I do know your tongue.

Lorenzo

Lorenzo, and thy love.

Jessica

Lorenzo, certain; and my love indeed,
For who love I so much? And now who knows   30
But you, Lorenzo, whether I am yours?

Lorenzo

Heaven and thy thoughts are witness that thou art.

Jessica

Here, catch this casket; it is worth the pains.
I am glad 'tis night, you do not look on me,
For I am much asham'd of my exchange:[15]
But love is blind, and lovers cannot see
The pretty follies that themselves commit;
For if they could, Cupid[16] himself would blush
To see me thus transformed to a boy.

Jessica is embarrassed.

Lorenzo

Descend, for you must be my torch-bearer.   40

Jessica

What! must I hold a candle to my shames?
They in themselves, good sooth,[17] are too too light.[18]
Why, 'tis an office of discovery, love,
And I should be obscur'd.[19]

Lorenzo

    So are you, sweet,
Even in the lovely garnish[20] of a boy,
But come at once;
For the close night doth play the runaway,
And we are stay'd[21] for at Bassanio's feast.

Jessica

I will make fast[22] the doors, and gild[23] myself
With some more ducats, and be with you straight.   50

                    [Exit above

Gratiano

Now, by my hood,[24] a gentle,[25] and no Jew.

Lorenzo

Beshrew[26] me, but I love her heartily;
For she is wise, if I can judge of her:

---

[15]change of clothes

[16]the Roman god of love

[17]indeed
[18]apparent
[19]hidden

[20]dress

[21]waited

[22]lock
[23]adorn with gold

[24]upon my word
[25]a pun on 'gentile': also 'gentle lady'
[26]curse: a mild oath

And fair she is, if that mine eyes be true;
And true she is, as she hath prov'd herself;
And therefore, like herself, wise, fair, and true,
Shall she be placed in my constant soul.

Declares his love for Jessica

Enter Jessica

What, art thou come? On, gentlemen; away!
Our masquing mates by this time for us stay.

[Exeunt, except Gratiano

Enter Antonio

Antonio

Who's there?   60

Gratiano

Signior Antonio!

Antonio

Fie, fie, Gratiano! where are all the rest?
'Tis nine o'clock; our friends all stay[27] for you.
No masque tonight: the wind is come about;[28]
Bassanio presently[29] will go aboard:
I have sent twenty out to seek for you.

Gratiano

I am glad on't: I desire no more delight
Than to be under sail and gone tonight.   [Exeunt

[28]wait

[28]has changed direction

[29]at once

Summary

The Elopement

Gratiano and Salerio are dressed for the masque and waiting for Lorenzo outside Shylock's house. To their surprise, Lorenzo is late for his rendezvous with Jessica. This prompts Gratiano and Salerio into commenting upon the usual enthusiasm of young lovers and the way that nothing ever quite lives up to its promise.

Lorenzo finally arrives, makes his apologies and calls to Jessica who appears on the balcony somewhat self-consciously dressed as a boy. Before decending, she passes down a casket full of money and jewels. She is not very keen, however, to be Lorenzo's torch-bearer: she is already self-conscious enough and feels that her disguise may not stand up to that much illumination. Having been reassured by Lorenzo, she helps herself to some more of Shylock's money before locking the doors as he had instructed. As she makes her way down, Lorenzo tells us how much he loves her.

As the lovers and friends set off, Antonio catches up with Gratiano who has lagged behind the others. Antonio announces that the masque has been called off; the wind has changed and Bassanio has decided to sail at once. Gratiano is not in the least unhappy at the prospect of being underway to Belmont.

Scene Analysis

Scene VI brings to its full development the sub-plot of Lorenzo and Jessica's elopement. Having done that, it points us back to the main story which is soon to be continued.

The bright masquers' uniforms and the tone of mischievous fun in the conversation of the lovers lends the scene a festive atmosphere. There are, however, some uneasy undercurrents. One of these is the extent to which the

> ' ... lovers cannot see
> The pretty follies that themselves commit;'

Jessica's 'kindness' to Lorenzo is matched with an equal callousness towards her father.

There is much talk too of disillusionment, of the extent to which

> '...All things that are,
> Are with more spirit chased than enjoy'd.'

And when the images chosen to express this disillusionment stray into talk of ships at the mercy of the 'strumpet wind' returning like the 'prodigal'

> 'With over-weather'd ribs and ragged sails,'

we are reminded of Antonio's argosies and the prodigal Bassanio and of the note of impending doom which we may have forgotten amidst the gaiety of young Venetians playing 'thieves for wives'. The fun is over for the moment, the masque is cancelled; 'the wind is come about' and the weather-vane points to Belmont and more serious business.

The Elizabethan Theatre

Two elements of the scene are worth commenting on for the light they throw on the theatre of Shakespeare's time. Firstly, Gratiano's words:

> 'This is the penthouse under which Lorenzo
> Desir'd us to make stand.'

tells us that the kind of theatre Shakespeare was writing for usually had a balcony or upper stage so that action could take place at two levels. It is a device which we associate readily with *Romeo and Juliet*.

A second noteworthy feature is that Jessica dresses in the 'garnish of a boy' and protests herself 'much asham'd' of the 'exchange'.

This is somewhat amusing when one considers that in Shakespeare's time all girls' roles were played by young boys whose voices had not yet broken: many of the great actors of the time served their apprenticeship playing female roles. And, of course, if girls are being played by boys it is very easy for them to be *'thus transformed to a boy again!'* It is a device of which we have not seen the last.

But come at once;
For the close night doth play the runaway,
And we are stay'd for at Bassanio's feast.   (Lorenzo, Act 2, Sc VI)

Characters

Another short scene full of action affords little scope for the development of character. The exception is perhaps the young couple who are the centre of the scene. **Gratiano**, as we might expect, does most of the talking as he waits for Lorenzo in the continually elegant presence of **Salerio** for whom a classical illusion to Venus is but everyday conversation. **Antonio** typically arrives when the fun is over and remains on the periphery of things.

JESSICA AND LORENZO

It is the young couple's big moment and they rise to the occasion. Jessica comes out of her shell, as it were, and Lorenzo is ever so satisfied with his lot. They are obviously in love but there is more than a little irony in Jessica's remark that:

> '...love is blind, and lovers cannot see
> The pretty follies that themselves commit;'

Lorenzo finds Jessica to be *'wise'* and *'fair'* and *'true'*, but a more detached observer might have some qualms about his choice of words. She is certainly not *'true'* to Shylock for whose trust and whose treasures she shows an unscrupulously callous attitude:

> *'I will make fast the doors, and gild myself*
> *With some more ducats, and be with you straight'.*

Nor does Lorenzo find anything wrong with this aspect of playing *'thieves for wives'*, even if he has the grace not to mention the *'casket'* that is *'worth the pains'*.

The romantic atmosphere that surrounds the young couple cannot obliterate the fact that Jessica is not only stealing but breaking religious ties and family bonds and that Lorenzo is her accomplice and the main beneficiary of the collusion.

Scene VII

Belmont. A room in Portia's house.
Enter Portia, with the Prince of Morocco and their Servants

Portia

¹reveal

²different

Go, draw aside the curtains, and discover[1]
The several[2] caskets to this noble prince.

[The curtains are drawn back

Now make your choice.

Morocco

The first, of gold, who this inscription bears:
'Who chooseth me shall gain what many men desire;'
The second, silver, which this promise carries:
'Who chooseth me shall get as much as he deserves;'
This third, dull lead, with warning all as blunt:
'Who chooseth me must give and hazard all he hath.'
How shall I know if I do choose the right?   *10*

Portia

The one of them contains my picture, prince:

³as well

If you choose that, then I am yours withal.[3]

Morocco

Some god direct my judgment! Let me see:
I will survey th' inscriptions back again:
What says this leaden casket?
'Who chooseth me must give and hazard all he hath.'
Must give! For what? for lead? hazard for lead?

This casket threatens. Men that hazard all
Do it in hope of fair advantages:
A golden mind stoops not to shows of dross;[4]   20   [4]rubbish
I'll then nor give nor hazard aught for lead.
What says the silver with her virgin[5] hue?[6]   [5]pure
'Who chooseth me shall get as much as he deserves'.   [6]colour
As much as he deserves! Pause there, Morocco,
And weigh thy value with an even hand.
If thou be'st rated[7] by thy estimation,   [7]valued
Thou dost deserve enough; and yet enough
May not extend so far as to the lady:
And yet to be afeard of my deserving
Were but a weak disabling of myself.   30
As much as I deserve! Why, that's the lady:
I do in birth deserve her, and in fortunes,
In graces, and in qualities of breeding;
But more than these, in love I do deserve.
What if I stray'd no further, but chose here?
Let's see once more this saying grav'd in gold:
'Who chooseth me shall gain what many men desire'.
Why, that's the lady: all the world desires her;
From the four corners of the earth they come,
To kiss this shrine, this mortal[8] breathing saint: 40   [8]living
The Hyrcanian[9] deserts and the vasty[10] wilds   [9]a region southeast of the
Of wide Arabia are as throughfares now   Caspian Sea
For princes to come view fair Portia: [10]immense
The watery kingdom,[11] whose ambitious head   [11]the ocean
Spits in the face of heaven, is no bar
To stop the foreign spirits, but they come,
As o'er a brook, to see fair Portia.
One of these three contains her heavenly picture.
Is't like[12] that lead contains her? T'were damnation   [12]likely
To think so base a thought: it were too gross[13]   50   [13]crude
To rib[14] her cerecloth[15] in the obscure grave.   [14]enclose
Or shall I think in silver she's immur'd.[16]   [15]shroud
Being ten times undervalu'd to tried gold?   [16]walled in
O sinful thought! Never so rich a gem
Was set in worse than gold. They have in England
A coin that bears the figure of an angel
Stamp'd in gold, but that's insculp'd[17] upon;   [17]engraved
But here an angel in a golden bed
Lies all within. Deliver me the key:
Here do I choose, and thrive I as I may!   60

Portia

There, take it, prince; and if my form lie there,
Then I am yours.

[He unlocks the golden casket

Morocco

    O hell! what have we here?
A carrion Death[18] within whose empty eye
There is a written scroll. I'll read the writing.
   All that glisters is not gold;
   Often have you heard that told:
   Many a man his life hath sold
   But my outside to behold:
   Gilded tombs do worms infold.[19]
   Had you been as wise as bold,   70
   Young in limbs, in judgment old,
   Your answer had not been inscroll'd[20]
   Fare you well, your suit is cold.[21]

Cold, indeed; and labour lost:
Then farewell heat, and welcome, frost!
Portia, adieu. I have too griev'd a heart
To take a tedious leave: thus losers part.

[Exit with his Servants

Portia

A gentle riddance. Draw the curtains: go.
Let all of his complexion choose me so.   *[Exeunt*

[18]skull

[19]contain

[20]written on a scroll
[21]has failed

Summary

Morocco Makes His Choice

The scene changes to Belmont where the Prince of Morocco comes to make his choice at the caskets. There are three caskets, one each of gold, silver and lead. Each casket bears an ambiguous inscription which the prince tries to puzzle out. Only one casket contains the picture of Portia and whoever chooses that casket will win her.

Morocco goes back over the inscriptions again, weighing the implications of what they say and searching for clues. He concludes that the golden casket is the most fitting container for Portia's image and that the inscription on it is most appropriate.

It is, however, the wrong casket and the wrong choice: it contains only a skull and a scroll suggesting that one should not judge by external appearances.

Morocco knows that his hopes are dashed and he wastes no time in making his departure. Portia is relieved.

Scene Analysis

The Caskets

At long last we see the famous caskets that we have heard so much about and we learn the details of the competition that will decide Portia's future. There are three kinds of casket, one each of gold, silver and lead, and each of them has an inscription whose significance is underlined by the fact that Morocco repeats them for effect. Whichever one Morocco chooses will obviously tell us something of his character.

That Morocco has a one-in-three chance of success lends the scene its air of palpable tension. It effects Portia particularly who does not know yet which casket contains her miniature portrait. She is unusually quiet and allows Morocco a long, hesitant speech which can only add to our suspense — a suspense which is in turn heightened by the sheer plausability of Morocco's argument that:

> '...Never so rich a gem
> Was set in worse than gold.'

> But here an angel in a golden bed
> Lies all within. Deliver me the key:
> Here do I choose, and thrive as I may!   (Prince of Morocco, Act 2, Sc VII)

He is wrong, however, and we breathe a sigh of relief even if the unwritten rules of romantic comedy had not allowed us totally to suspend the belief that anyone other than Bassanio should win Portia's hand.

Even if wrong, however, Morocco's choice is rich in symbolism and the answer it evokes touches on one of the favouite themes in all of Shakespeare's plays and poetry. Morocco has judged by external appearances and the skull inside the golden casket symbolises the death and failure that comes to those who so choose:

> *'All that glisters is not gold...*
> *Gilded tombs do worms infold.'*

It is one of Shakespeare's great themes, expressed perhaps most beautifully in his sonnets, that the wealth and sensory beauty that gold symbolises are but transitory and that permanence and eternity are only to be found in things of the heart. It is in some ways the theme of this play and bodes ill for Shylock whose obsession is material wealth and whose god is gold.

Characters

THE PRINCE OF MOROCCO

Morocco reveals himself to us through his reaction to the different caskets and the inscriptions they bear. The proud prince portrayed in Act 2, Scene I dismisses the lead casket because it is *'so base a thought'* and somehow beneath his dignity:

> *'A golden mind stoops not to shows of dross;'*

He knows he must *"hazard all he hath"* but does not consider lead worthy of the risks involved:

> *'I'll then nor give nor hazard aught for lead.'*

He cannot dismiss the silver casket so easily, however. The inscription —*'Who chooseth me shall get as much as he deserves.'* – appeals to Morocco's high sense of self-esteem. Morocco knows his own worth:

> *'I do in birth deserve her, and in fortunes,*
> *In graces, and in qualities of breeding;*
> *But more than these, in love I do deserve.'*

There is a chink in his armour, however; the niggling doubt of a black man in a white racialist society who fears that he may not be 'rated' quite according to his own *'estimation'* of himself. We remember his opening remarks in Scene I,

> 'Mislike me not for my complexion,'

and note the circumspection here that he may not be worthy:

> 'Thou dost deserve enough; and yet enough
> May not extend so far as to the lady:'

It would therefore appear to be the discomfort caused by a latent inferiority complex that prompts Morocco to *'stray ... further'* rather than *'choosing the silver casket'*.

It is not surprising that *'tried gold'* should appeal most to a man who considers himself to have a *'golden mind'*. What Morocco reveals here is perhaps a barbaric sense of values that makes simple and straightforward calculations on the basis of external appearances, and for which silver is *'ten times undervalu'd to tried gold'*.

It is ironic that in so choosing by externals Morocco is exercising his judgement in the one way he had specifically asked Portia not to judge him. His disappointment is total and unqualified:

> 'O hell! what have we here?'

Nothing in Morocco's role becomes him quite so well as the way he leaves the stage. He takes failure with admirable dignity and gains in defeat our sympathy and respect:

> 'Portia, adieu. I have too griev'd a heart
> To take a tedious leave: thus losers part.'

He has made an impression upon us quite out of proportion to his role and the two short scenes given him. It is clear too that this colourful and exotic alien retained a grip on Shakespeare's imagination for he returned to the stage and to Venice years later through his creator's pen in the guise of Othello. *Othello* could be seen as one possible answer to the fascinating question: 'What if Morocco had chosen the casket containing Portia's picture?'

PORTIA

Portia has very little to say for herself in this scene other than to reiterate her loyalty to the device of the caskets. Anxiety about the outcome of Morocco's choice reduces her for the most part to silence.

Morocco tells us, however, what a desirable and sought-after young lady she is:

> 'all the world desires her;
> From the four corners of the earth they come...
> The Hyrcanian deserts and the vasty wilds
> Of wide Arabia are as thoroughfares now
> For princes to come view fair Portia.'

Portia instils Morocco with such awe that he sees her as a *'mortal breathing saint'* whose *'heavenly picture'* is like *'an angel in a golden bed'*. Shakespeare is not given to hagiography, however, and Portia's final remark,

> *'Let all of his complexion choose me so.'*

reflects an author who, if he cannot allow Shylock to be a total devil, equally cannot allow Portia to be the total saint that Morocco thinks she is.

Scene VIII

Venice. A street. Enter Salerio, and Solanio

Salerio

Why, man, I saw Bassanio under sail,
With him is Gratiano gone along;
And in their ship I am sure Lorenzo is not.

Solanio

The villain Jew with outcries rais'd the duke,
Who went with him to search Bassanio's ship.

Salerio

He came too late, the ship was under sail,
But there the duke was given to understand
That in a gondola were seen together
Lorenzo and his amorous[1] Jessica.
Besides, Antonio certified[2] the duke   10
They were not with Bassanio in his ship.

[1] loving
[2] assured

Solanio

I never heard a passion so confus'd,
So strange, outrageous, and so variable,
As the dog Jew did utter in the streets:
'My daughter! O my ducats! O my daughter!
Fled with a Christian! O my Christian ducats!
Justice! the law! my ducats, and my daughter!
A sealed bag, two sealed bags of ducats,
Of double ducats, stol'n from me by my daughter!
And jewels! two stones, two rich and precious
        stones,   20
Stol'n by my daughter! Justice! find the girl!
She hath the stones upon her, and the ducats.'

Salerio

Why, all the boys of Venice follow him,
Crying his stones, his daughter, and his ducats.

Solanio

Let good Antonio look he keep his day,[3]
Or he shall pay for this.

[3] pay his debt by the agreed date

Salerio

       Marry, well remember'd.
I reason'd[4] with a Frenchman yesterday,
Who told me, in the narrow seas that part
The French and English, there miscarried[5]
A vessel of our country richly fraught.[6]   30
I thought upon Antonio when he told me,
And wish'd in silence that it were not his.

[4] talked

[5] was wrecked
[6] laden

Solanio

You were best to tell Antonio what you hear;
Yet do not suddenly, for it may grieve him.

Salerio

A kinder gentleman treads not the earth.
I saw Bassanio and Antonio part:
Bassanio told him he would make some speed
Of his return: he answer'd, 'Do not so;
Slubber[7] not business for my sake, Bassanio,
But stay the very riping of the time,[8]   40
And for the Jew's bond which he hath of me,
Let it not enter in your mind of love:
Be merry, and employ your chiefest thoughts
To courtship and such fair ostents[9] of love
As shall conveniently become you there.'
And even there, his eye being big with tears,
Turning his face, he put his hand behind him,
And with affection wondrous sensible[10]
He wrung Bassanio's hand; and so they parted.

[7] rush
[8] as long as it takes

[9] displays

[10] tender

Solanio

I think he only loves the world for him.   50
I pray thee, let us go and find him out,
And quicken his embraced heaviness[11]
With some delight or other.

[11] the sadness which he clings to

Salerio

      Do we so.

Summary

The Aftermath Of The Elopement

On a street in Venice, Salerio and Solanio are discussing recent developments. Bassanio and Gratiano have departed for Belmont but mystery surrounds the whereabouts of Lorenzo and Jessica. Shylock has found out about the elopement and the loss of his money and he has not taken it lightly. He has called out the authorities to search Bassanio's ship but it has been a vain effort as the ship has already sailed.

To cover Lorenzo and Jessica's tracks, a story has been put out that they were seen in a gondola and Antonio has given his word to the Duke that they are not on Bassanio's ship.

Shylock, we hear, cannot contain his anger and shock. He is going about in the streets raving about his money, his daughter and his jewels — unable in his confusion to decide which loss hurts him most. He is being taunted and baited by the young boys of Venice.

Solanio is worried that Shylock may take it all out on Antonio if Antonio fails to repay his loan on time. Salerio furnishes us with the ominous news of a shipwreck and the possibility that it may be one of Antonio's ships. It is decided that the news should be broken to Antonio gently.

The scene ends with a description of the emotional parting of Antonio and Bassanio. Salerio praises Antonio's selflessness and lest he be indulging in his loneliness again they set off to find him and cheer him up.

Scene Analysis

Scene VIII gives the impression of many things happening and of time passing. Bassanio and Gratiano are *'under sail'* for Belmont and there is little doubt but that Lorenzo and Jessica are with them. Shylock has discovered the elopement of his daughter and the theft of his ducats and jewels. There are ominous implications for Antonio in Shylock's crazed derangement and in the reported shipwreck. Finally, we learn of the manner in which Antonio and Bassanio parted.

Reported Happenings

It is interesting that these events are not portrayed on stage but are merely reported to us through the dramatic narrative (dialogue) of Salerio and Solanio. Scene VIII is not so much one scene as a series of small scenes or vignettes reported second hand.

The two most significant of these reported scenes involve the reaction of Shylock to his triple loss, and Antonio's parting with Bassanio. There is an obvious contrast in the manner in which these incidents are portrayed. Shylock's predicament is presented in a tone of scornful amusement, while Bassanio's leave-taking of Antonio is described with sympathy and compassion.

The Dramatic Intentions Of The Scene

The contrast in the manner in which Antonio and Shylock are presented reveals the dramatic intention of the scene which is to engage our sympathy and affection for Antonio while enlisting our scorn for Shylock: the main thrust of the play requires that Shylock be a villain.

Why, all the boys of Venice follow him,
Crying his stones, his daughter, and his ducats.   (Salerio, Act 2, Sc VIII)

An Interesting Question

Why, we wonder, did Shakespeare not present on stage two scenes so rich in dramatic potential? Reflecting on and answering this question gives us an insight into the craftsmanship of a master-playwright. The answer must be that a presentation of these scenes on stage might take from the dramatic intention of the scene as a whole. It would be difficult to contain our sympathy for Shylock if we observed his distress and especially the way in which *'all the boys in Venice'* taunted and baited him. Reporting it second hand takes the sting out of it and allows Shakespeare to introduce a tone of ridicule and amusement through the voice of the reporter.

There was a similar danger in a presentation of Antonio's emotion:

> '*And even there, his eye being big with tears,*
> *Turning his face, he put his hand behind him,*
> *And with affection wondrous sensible*
> *He wrung Bassanio's hand...*'

This scene is potentially mawkish and embarrassing and is better at one remove and as interpreted through the agency of Salerio's favourable tone.

Characters

SALERIO AND SOLANIO

While Salerio and Solanio are the only two characters to appear on stage in this scene, their role is not so much to reveal themselves as to inform us of developments in the plot and to throw light on Shylock and Antonio on whose misfortunes they have widely contrasting attitudes. The function of Salerio and Solanio is akin to the role of a chorus in Greek and medieval drama.

SHYLOCK

Shylock, we hear, has not borne his losses tamely. His first resort was to '*justice*' and '*the law*', reflecting a craving for law he will return to in later scenes: Shylock insists on the rights of aliens in Venice and their equality under the law. He is initially successful in that he '*rais'd the duke ... to search Bassanio's ship*'. He is soon to be frustrated, however; Bassanio's ship is gone and there is a conspiracy of silence to stonewall the '*villain Jew*' and cover the tracks of '*Lorenzo and his amorous Jessica*'.

The duke has been '*given to understand*' that '*They were not with Bassanio in his ship*' but rather '*in a gondola were seen together*'. Shylock has been robbed and no one will tell him the truth. He goes mad with frustration and in his agony and despair makes no differentiation between '*his stones, his daughter and his ducats*'.

He loses control and falls into:

> '*...a passion so confus'd.*
> *So strange, outrageous, and so variable...*'

that he is reduced to raving incoherently in the streets and is mocked mercilessly by '*all the boys in Venice*'.

While Shylock's treatment in the streets might raise our sympathy for him, the overall impact of this scene is to portray him as a villain in whose misfortune his fellow Venetians can rejoice. The '*dog Jew*' becomes such an object of sport and merriment that pity for him is made to appear inappropriate. Shylock has been made to look ridiculous in his absence to a degree that would not have been possible in his presence.

Shylock now has a three-fold motive for revenge against Antonio. Antonio's inextricable association with Shylock's losses is now added to the commercial rivalry and religious differences that generated hatred in the past. Jessica has *'Fled with a Christian'* who is associated with Antonio and they are – Shylock suspects and everyone else presumes – on the ship chartered by Antonio's best friend and financed at Antonio's behest with Shylock's money. And Antonio has been part of the cover up!

> *'Besides, Antonio certified the duke*
> *They were not with Bassanio in his ship.'*

It is not difficult to anticipate Shylock's mind when next he enters upon the stage.

ANTONIO

If Shylock is a 'loser' in Scene VIII, so too is Antonio. But whereas Shylock's misfortunes engender ridicule, Antonio's worries are presented in a manner calculated to raise our concern and affection for him.

We have good reason to be concerned for Antonio. He has been legally cornered by Shylock who is now deranged and maniacal and who has, as we have seen, every reason to seek out revenge. Solanio sees the obvious:

> *'Let good Antonio look to keep his day,*
> *Or he shall pay for this.'*

That Antonio may not be able to *'keep his day'* is suggested more forcibly now in the images of *'narrow seas'* that have been carefully nurtured through various scenes. There is an unmistakeable suggestion in Solanio's ominous words that the worst has happened:

> *'there miscarried*
> *A vessel of our country richly fraught.'*

Solanio's solicitude does nothing to alleviate our fears:

> *'You were best to tell Antonio what you hear;*
> *Yet do not suddenly, for it may grieve him.'*

If the misfortune we fear is coming Antonio's way, it could not be happening to a nicer person.

> *'A kinder gentleman treads not the earth.'*

Salerio eulogises Antonio's personal qualities: Antonio is unselfish, genuine and affectionate. He wants Bassanio to leave the problems of Venice far behind when he goes to woo Portia:

> 'And for the Jew's bond which he hath of me,
> Let it not enter in your mind of love:'

He simply wishes his friend to have a good time:

> '"Be merry and employ your chiefest thoughts
> To courtship and such fair ostents of love
> As shall conveniently become you there."'

Antonio, it appears, values friendshiip above everything else: he 'only loves the world' for his friend Bassanio. This is a sharp contrast to Shylock who values even his daughter in terms of possession and whose joy is 'jewels' and 'ducats'.

As the scene ends it appears that Antonio has given in again to that morbid strain of melancholy in his character in which we encountered him when the play opened. But he still attracts the loyalty and solicitude of his friends who set out to 'quicken his embraced heaviness.'

Scene IX

Belmont A room in Portia's house.
Enter Nerissa, with a Servant

Nerissa

Quick, quick, I pray thee; draw the curtain straight:[1]
The Prince of Arragon hath ta'en his oath,
And comes to his election[2] presently.[3]

> [Curtains drawn to reveal caskets

Enter the Prince of Arragon, Portia and Servants

Portia

Behold, there stand the caskets, noble prince:
If you choose that wherein I am contain'd,
Straight shall our nuptial rites be solemniz'd;[4]
But if you fail, without more speech, my lord,
You must be gone from hence immediately.

Arragon

I am enjoin'd[5] by oath to observe three things:
First, never to unfold[6] to any one   *10*
Which casket 'twas I chose; next, if I fail
Of the right casket, never in my life

[1] at once
[2] choice
[3] now

[4] we will be married immediately

[5] bound
[6] disclose

To woo a maid in way of marriage; lastly,
If I do fail in fortune of my choice,
Immediately to leave you and be gone.

Portia

To these injunctions[7] every one doth swear   [7]conditions
That comes to hazard for my worthless self.

Arragon

And so have I address'd me.[8] Fortune now   [8]faced up to
To my heart's hope! Gold, silver, and base lead.
'Who chooseth me must give and hazard all he hath.'   20
You shall look fairer, ere I give or hazard.
What says the golden chest? ha! let me see:
'Who chooseth me shall gain what many men desire'.
What many men desire! that 'many' may be meant
By the fool multitude, that choose by show,
Not learning more than the fond[9] eye doth teach,   [9]foolish
Which pries[10] not to th'interior, but, like the martlet[11]   [10]searches
                                                                [11]the house-martin
Builds in the weather on the outward wall,   [12]in the path of likely
Even in the force and road of casualty.[12]   accidents
I will not choose what many men desire,   30
Because I will not jump[13] with common spirits   [13]go along with
And rank me with the barbarous multitudes.
Why, then to thee, thou silver treasure-house;
Tell me once more what title thou dost bear:
Who chooseth me shall get as much as he deserves'.
And well said too; for who shall go about
To cozen[14] fortune, and be honourable   [14]cheat
Without the stamp of merit? Let none presume
To wear an undeserved dignity.
O that estates,[15] degrees,[16] and offices[17]   40   [15]titles
Were not deriv'd[18] corruptly,[19] and that clear honour   [16]social position; status
Were purchas'd[20] by the merit of the wearer.   [17]official appointments
How many then should cover[21] that stand bare!   [18]obtained
How many be commanded that command!   [19]by foul means
                                                                [20]earned or bought
How much low peasantry would then be glean'd[22]   [21]keep their hats on
From the true seed of honour! and how much honour   [22]picked out
Pick'd from the chaff and ruin of the times[23]   [23]outcasts
To be new varnish'd! Well, but to my choice:
'Who chooseth me shall get as much as he deserves'.
I will assume desert.[24] Give me a key for this,   50   [24]deserving
And instantly unlock my fortunes here.

                        [*He opens the silver casket*

Portia

Too long a pause for that which you find there.

Arragon

What's here? the portrait of a blinking idiot,
Presenting me a schedule[25]! I will read it.
How much unlike art thou to Portia!
How much unlike my hopes and my deservings!
'Who chooseth me shall have as much as he deserves'.
Did I deserve no more than a fool's head?
Is that my prize? are my deserts no better?

Portia

To offend, and judge, are distinct offices,   60
And of opposed natures.

Arragon

     What is here?
The fire seven times tried this:
Seven times tried that judgment is
That did never choose amiss.
Some there be that shadows kiss:
Such have but a shadow's bliss.
There be fools alive, iwis,[26]
Silver'd o'er; and so was this.
Take what wife you will to bed,
I will ever be your head,   70
So be gone: you are sped.[27]

Still more fool I shall appear
By the time I linger here:
With one fool's head I came to woo,
But I go away with two.
Sweet, adieu. I'll keep my oath,
Patiently to bear my wrath.

           [Exit Arragon with his Servants

Portia

Thus hath the candle sing'd the moth.
O these deliberate fools! when they do choose,
They have the wisdom by their wit to lose.   80

Nerissa

The ancient saying is no heresy:
'Hanging and wiving[28] goes by destiny.'

Portia

Come, draw the curtain, Nerissa.

          Enter a Servant

Servant

Where is my lady?

Portia

     Here; what would my lord?

[25]scroll

[26]indeed

[27]finished

[28]marrying

Servant

Madam, there is alighted[29] at your gate
A young Venetian, one that comes before
To signify th'approaching of his lord;
From whom he bringeth sensible regreets,[30]
To wit,[31] besides commends[32] and courteous breath,
Gifts of rich value. Yet I have not seen   *90*
So likely an ambassador of love.
A day in April never came so sweet
To show how costly[33] summer was at hand,
As this fore-spurrer[34] comes before his lord.

Portia

No more, I pray thee: I am half afeard
Thou wilt say anon he is some kin[35] to thee,
Thou spend'st such high-day wit[36] in praising him.
Come, come, Nerissa; for I long to see
Quick Cupid's post[37] that comes so mannerly.

Nerissa

Bassanio, lord Love, if thy will it be!   *100* [Exeunt

[29]has landed

[30]tangible greeting, i.e. gifts
[31]that is to say
[32]compliments

[33]rich
[34]advance messenger

[35]relation
[36]special cleverness

[37]messenger

Summary

A Spanish Prince

It is time for another of Portia's suitors to take his chance at the caskets. This time it is the Prince of Arragon. Like anyone else who wishes to try the caskets, Arragon has sworn to keep three promises: he will keep his choice of casket a secret and if he chooses wrongly he will forego marriage forever and leave immediately.

Like Morocco before him, Arragon thinks aloud as he ponders the three caskets and their inscriptions. And like Morocco he wastes no time on the commonality of ugly lead. He finds gold common too since it panders to popular taste: Arragon does not want to be associated with the common desires of the vulgar mob. He regards himself as a true-born nobleman and regrets that so many low-born peasants now swell the ranks of the nobility. He finds the inscription on the silver casket most appropriate to the degree of his deserving and he chooses it.

Arragon's dumbfounded pause indicates to Portia that he has chosen the wrong casket and indeed he has. He finds instead of Portia's image a scroll and a picture of a goggle-eyed fool. He asks if he did not deserve better than this and Portia replies that an offender is not allowed to judge his own case. Arragon reads from the scroll that perfect judgement must be as refined as silver and that fools embrace illusions instead of reality. Arragon feels very foolish and knows that the longer he stays the bigger fool he will appear.

When Arragon has left, Portia expresses contempt for the elaborate and futile deliberation which has defeated her suitors to date. Nerissa expresses the view enshrined in an old proverb that important things are decided by fate.

Finally, Portia learns that a young Venetian is at the gate with news that his master will soon arrive. The young man has made a very favourable impression on Portia's servants through his courteous behaviour and the valuable gifts he bears.

The scene ends with Nerissa's prayer that the approaching suitor be Bassanio.

Scene Analysis

We now know which casket contains Portia's miniature portrait. That much suspense is over but the burden of knowing what he must choose will only deepen suspense when Bassanio approaches the caskets.

We also know what frame of mind Bassanio must be in if he is to choose correctly. Morocco and Arragon have been defeated by excessive reasoning:

'O these deliberate fools! when they do choose,
They have the wisdom by their wit to lose.'

I will not choose what many men desire,
Because I will not jump with common spirits
And rank me with the barbarous multitudes.   (Prince of Arragon, Act 2, Sc IX)

We remember Nerissa's words in Act 1, Scene II, that the correct casket will

'Never be chosen by any rightly,
but one who you shall rightly love.'

Right choice depends not on reasoning but on love.

It will also depend, Nerissa tells us, on fate, for

> *'The ancient saying is no heresy:*
> *"Hanging and wiving goes by destiny."'*

And fate would appear to be on Bassanio's side. His competitors have chosen wrongly and the images that accompany his arrival in Belmont are unquestionably optimistic:

> *'A day in April never came so sweet*
> *To show how costly summer was at hand,*
> *As this fore-spurrer comes before his lord.'*

Such poetic speech surely anticipates the blissful harmony that destiny is about to unfold for Bassanio and Portia.

Characters

THE PRINCE OF ARRAGON

The Prince of Arragon is quite simply a snob. Arragon reminds us of 'arrogant' and that he certainly is. He is, in fact, so conceited that we are not surprised when he makes the wrong choice. He is a good example of pride before a fall.

Arragon's claim to Portia is that he comes from very noble ancestry. Nobility and merit are his hobby-horses and he believes that there are very few of his calibre left, even among the ranks of the nobility: *'low peasantry'* has broken ranks and presumes *'To wear an undeserved dignity'*.

Arragon is more subtle and prudent than Morocco who simply chose the obvious. Arragon's choice is equally flawed, however, since he is blinded by his own importance. His decision is based on the presumption of his superiority to the crowd:

> *'I will not choose what many men desire,*
> *Because I will not jump with common spirits*
> *And rank me with the barbarous multitudes.'*

The trouble with the *'fool multitude'*, as Arragon sees it, is that they:

> *'...choose by show,*
> *Not learning more than the fond eye doth teach,*
> *Which pries not to th' interior...'*

The irony is that Arragon fails to live by his own maxims. He too *'pries not to th' interior'* because his decision is devoid of love and has nothing to do with the heart.

There is no evidence that Arragon has any love or affection for Portia. Unlike Morocco he makes no effort to express his love for her; he never even mentions her name. He uses reasoning only in his choice and becomes, in Portia's eyes, the *'deliberate fool'* who by his *'wisdom'* has the *'wit to lose'*.

There is no doubt that Shakespeare's first audience would have taken great pleasure in Arragon's discomfiture, not only because he was an arrogant snob, but also because he was Spanish. It must be remembered that the Armada was very recent history when this play was written and that to its first audience Spain meant Philip, the Inquisition and war. Although the Spanish grandee was a familiar figure of derision on the Elizabethan stage, Arragon is the only Spanish character in all of Shakespeare's writings.

PORTIA

Portia faces a new chapter in the *'lottery'* of her *'destiny'* with grace and courage and continuing loyalty to her father's will. She tells Arragon:

> *'If you choose that wherein I am contain 'd,*
> *Straight shall our nuptial rights be solemniz'd;'*

Though she is the object now of Arragon's *'hazard'* and is considered worthy of the penalties that accompany an incorrect choice, she considers herself with disarming **humility**:

> *'To these injunctions every one doth swear*
> *That comes to hazard for my worthless self.'*

Her **tension** and suspense are evident in the sharpness with which she interprets Arragon's speechless reaction on opening the silver casket:

> *'Too long a pause for that which you find there.'*

The legal tone of her next lines anticipates the judicial role she will play in a later scene:

> *'To offend, and judge, are distinct offices,*
> *And of opposed natures.'*

She recognises the fatal fascination with reasoning that has defeated Morocco and Arragon:

> *'Thus hath the candle sing'd the moth.'*

The implication in her words is that right choice depends not on reasoning but on love.

> *'O these deliberate fools! when they do choose,*
> *They have the wisdom by their wit to lose.'*

Portia is initially sceptical at the glowing reports of the new suitor.

> *'No more, I pray thee: I am half afeard*
> *Thou wilt say anon he is some kin to thee,*
> *Thou spend'st such high-day wit in praising him.'*

Her curiosity has been roused, however, and there is a hint of impatience as well as anticipation in her closing remark:

> *'Come, come, Nerissa; for I long to see*
> *Quick Cupid's post that comes so mannerly.'*

Act 3

Scene I

Venice. A Street. Enter Solanio, and Salerio

Solanio

Now, what news on the Rialto?

Salerio

Why, yet it lives there[1] unchecked[2] that Antonio hath
a ship of rich lading[3] wrecked on the narrow seas;
the Goodwins,[4] I think they call the place, a very
dangerous flat, and fatal, where the carcasses of many
a tall ship lie buried, as they say, if my gossip
Report be an honest woman of her word.

Solanio

I would she were as lying a gossip in that as ever
knapped[5] ginger, or made her neighbours believe she
wept for the death of a third husband. But it is   10
true — without any slips of prolixity[6] or crossing the
plain highway of talk — that the good Antonio, the
honest Antonio — O, that I had a title good enough
to keep his name company!

Salerio

Come, the full stop.

Solanio

Ha! what say'st thou? Why, the end is, he hath
lost a ship.

Salerio

I would it might prove the end of his losses.

Solanio

Let me say 'amen' betimes,[7] lest the devil cross my
prayer, for here he comes in the likeness of a Jew.   20

Enter Shylock

How now, Shylock! what news among the merchants?

Shylock

You knew, none so well, none so well as you, of my
daughter's flight.

Salerio

That's certain: I, for my part, knew the tailor that made
the wings she flew withal.[8]

[1] it is rumoured
[2] uncontradicted
[3] cargo
[4] the Goodwin Sands off the coast of Kent

[5] bit off

[6] verbosity

[7] immediately

[8] with

[9]feathered
[10]nature
[11]mother

Solanio

And Shylock, for his own part, knew the bird was
fledge,[9] and then it is the complexion[10] of them all to
leave the dam.[11]

Shylock

She is damned for it.

Salerio

That's certain, if the devil may be her judge.   30

Shylock

My own flesh and blood to rebel!

Solanio

[12]dead flesh

Out upon it, old carrion![12] rebels it at these years?

Shylock

I say my daughter is my flesh and my blood.

Salerio

There is more difference between thy flesh and hers
than between jet and ivory; more between your bloods

[13]the Rhine Valley was
famous for its white wines

than there is between red wine and Rhenish.[13]
But tell us, do you hear whether Antonio have had any
loss at sea or no?

Shylock

There I have another bad match: a bankrupt, a
prodigal, who dare scarce show his head on the   40
Rialto; a beggar, that was used to come so smug upon

[14]market-place
[15]accustomed

the mart.[14] Let him look to his bond! he was wont[15]
to call me usurer. Let him look to his bond! he was
wont to lend money for a Christian courtesy. Let him
look to his bond!

Salerio

Why, I am sure, if he forfeit thou wilt not take his flesh:
what's that good for?

Shylock

To bait fish withal: if it will feed nothing else,
it will feed my revenge. He hath disgraced me, and
hindered me half a million, laughed at my losses,   50
mocked at my gains, scorned my nation, thwarted my
bargains, cooled my friends, heated mine
enemies; and what's his reason? I am a Jew. Hath
not a Jew eyes? hath not a Jew hands, organs,

[16]limbs

dimensions[16] senses, affections, passions? fed with
the same food, hurt with the same weapons, subject
to the same diseases, healed by the same means,

warmed and cooled by the same winter and summer, as
a Christian is?
If you prick us, do we not bleed?
if you tickle us, do we not laugh? if you poison us,   *60*
do we not die? andif you wrong us, shall we not
revenge? If we are like you in the rest, we will
resemble you in that. If a Jew wrong a Christian,
what is his humility? Revenge! If a Christian
wrong a Jew, what should his sufferance be[17] by   [17]what should he endure
Christian example? Why, revenge! The villainy you
teach me I will execute, and it shall go hard but   [18]improve upon
I will better[18] the instruction.[19]   [19]the example

Enter a Servant

Servant

Gentlemen, my master Antonio is at his house, and
desires to speak with you both.   *70*

Salerio

We have been up and down to seek him.

Enter Tubal

Solanio

Here comes another of the tribe: a third cannot be
matched, unless the devil himself turn Jew.

[Exeunt Solanio, Salerio and Servant

Shylock

How now, Tubal! what news from Genoa? Hast thou
found my daughter?

Tubal

I often came where I did hear of her, but cannot find her.

Shylock

Why there, there, there, there! a diamond gone,
cost me two thousand ducats in Frankfurt! The curse
never fell upon our nation till now; I never felt it
till now: two thousand ducats in that, and other   *80*
precious, precious jewels. I would[20] my daughter   [20]wish
were dead at my foot, and the jewels in her ear!
would she were hearsed[21] at my foot, and the ducats   [21]coffined
in her coffin! No news of them — why so? and I know
not what's spent in the search. Why thou — loss upon
loss! the thief gone with so much, and so much to
find the thief; and no satisfaction, no revenge:
nor no ill luck stirring but what lights o'[22] my   [22]lands on

shoulders; no sighs but o' my breathing; no tears
but o' my shedding.   90

Tubal

Yes, other men have ill luck too. Antonio, as I
heard in Genoa —

Shylock

What, what, what? ill luck? ill luck?

Tubal

23wrecked

— hath an argosy cast away,23 coming from Tripolis.

Shylock

I thank God! I thank God! Is it true? is it true?

Tubal

I spoke with some of the sailors that escaped the wreck.

Shylock

I thank thee, good Tubal. Good news, good news!
ha, ha! Heard in Genoa?

Tubal

Your daughter spent in Genoa, as I heard, one
night, fourscore ducats.   100

Shylock

24at one go

Thou stick'st a dagger in me: I shall never see my
gold again: fourscore ducats at a sitting!24
fourscore ducats!

Tubal

25several
26go bankrupt

There came divers25 of Antonio's creditors in my
company to Venice, that swear he cannot choose but break.26

Shylock

I am very glad of it: I'll plague him; I'll torture
him: I am glad of it.

Tubal

One of them showed me a ring that he had of your
daughter for a monkey.

Shylock

27shame on

Out upon27 her! Thou torturest me, Tubal: it was my   110
turquoise; I had it of Leah when I was a bachelor:
I would not have given it for a wilderness of monkeys.

Tubal

But Antonio is certainly undone.

Shylock

28hire

Nay, that's true, that's very true. Go, Tubal, fee28

me an officer; bespeak²⁹ him a fortnight before. I   ²⁹book
will have the heart of him, if he forfeit; for, were
he out of Venice, I can make what merchandise³⁰ I   ³⁰profits
will. Go, Tubal, and meet me at our synagogue;
go, good Tubal; at our synagogue, Tubal.

[Exeunt in different directions

Summary

Shylock Is Baited And Consoled

Act 3 opens in Venice where Solanio and Salerio are discussing the continuing rumours about the loss of one of Antonio's ships. They fear that the rumours may be true and hope that Antonio's losses will at least go no further.

Shylock enters upon their conversation and accuses them of being accessories to Jessica's elopement. Their reaction is to pun on his words and to tease him. He reminds them that their friend Antonio had better fulfil his bond.

Salerio tests Shylock as to whether he would really pursue his pound of flesh in the event of Antonio being unable to repay his debt. Shylock says he would do so if only to use as bait for fishing, but mainly to satisfy his longing for revenge. He goes back over the wrongs Antonio has inflicted on him and makes an impassioned plea for tolerance of his race. Jews are, he tells us, as human as anyone else; they have the same feelings as Christians and when wronged they too can seek satisfaction in revenge.

Solanio and Salerio are called away suddenly to Antonio's house and as they leave, Shylock's friend and fellow Jew, Tubal, arrives. Tubal has been out looking for Jessica and is coming from Genoa where he has traced her without being able to find her.

Shylock bemoans his losses and sees his misfortunes as part of God's punishment of the Jewish nation. He wishes Jessica dead at his feet with his stolen ducats in her coffin. Shylock regrets not only his losses but the further costs he has incurred in trying to trace and get back what was his. It has all been to no avail and Shylock feels particularly hard done by.

Tubal interjects that Antonio has had bad luck too and Shylock cannot wait to hear more. As the story of the shipwreck unfolds, he is increasingly elated: he rejoices at the news and thanks God. Tubal plunges him back into depression, however, by interspersing news of Antonio's misfortune with snippets of information about the liberal way in which Jessica is squandering his fortune. That she should exchange for a monkey a ring which he had received from his dead wife goes particularly hard on him.

Tubal consoles Shylock once more with the certainty of Antonio's impending bankruptcy and is sent off to hire a sheriff's officer and have him ready to arrest Antonio the minute he forfeits the bond.

Scene Analysis

If there was little dramatic movement in the last scenes of Act 2, **matters now come to a head**. As news of Antonio's losses hardens, **the sense of crisis and foreboding mounts**. We remember Shylock's words in Act 1, Scene III:

> *'If I can catch him once upon the hip,*
> *I will feed fat the ancient grudge I bear him.'*

There came divers of Antonio's creditors in my
company to Venice, that swear he cannot choose but break.   *(Tubal, Act 3, Sc I)*

After the poetry of true love in the previous scene we are treated now to the prose of true hatred which emits from an increasingly malevolent Shylock. The scene divides into three distinct episodes:

(1) Solanio and Salerio's conversation (lines 1–20) acts as a chorus which keeps us up to date on what is happening. They convey to us the increasingly clear news:

> *'... that Antonio hath a ship of rich lading wrecked on the narrow seas—'*

(2) Solanio and Salerio's exchange with Shylock (lines 21–73) establishes the extent to which Shylock embodies the greatest threat of all to Antonio:

> *'... he was wont to call me usurer. Let him look to his bond!'*(3) The scene ends with the episode in which Shylock and Tubal are alone and intimate in their Jewish solidarity, even if Tubal takes malicious pleasure in torturing his countryman with alternate accounts of Antonio's losses and Jessica's wastefulness.

'Thou stick'st a dagger in me: I shall never see my
gold again: fourscore ducats at a sitting!
fourscore ducats!'

The Comic Perspective Restored

Despite the mounting tension, the scene as a whole is imbued with humour. Solanio's comparison of Shylock to the devil; Shylock's grotesque eagerness and delight at the news of Antonio's possible ruin; the manner in which Shylock's face and spirits plunge from elation to despair as Tubal tortures him; the humour of a vindictive miser's wealth being spent frivolously and a precious ring being given away for a monkey — all prompt us to laugh and this maintains the comic perspective in the face of gathering clouds.

Characters

The Two Dimensions Of Shylock

When Shylock intrudes upon the conversation of Solanio and Salerio we see him in person for the first time since the elopement of Jessica. We have been told of his mental disposition in the proceeding scenes, however, and are well prepared for the villainy of his intentions. But in a scene that is full of texture and dimension, we are never quite allowed to forget that the villain is also very human indeed. Villainy and humanity are the two poles within which Shylock orbits and he is rarely one without the other: he rarely engenders our revulsion without at the same time evoking a degree of our compassion. Both poles of his personality are well represented in this scene.

Shylock's Villainy

(1) Shylock's villainy derives in the first place from his **lust for revenge**. He is committed to the barbarous enterprise of getting a pound of Antonio's flesh, if only *'to bait fish withal'*. His real motive is totally explicit, however: *'it will feed my revenge'*. When Shylock hears of Antonio's plight, he is ecstatic:

   'I am very glad of it: I'll plague him; I'll torture him: I am glad of it.'

   He therefore leaves us in no doubt that he will be ruthless, vindictive and without mercy in his treatment of Antonio.

(2) There is something abhorrent in a man who is dismayed at his own misfortunes and at the same time overjoyed at the misfortunes of another.

(3) What most deprives Shylock of our sympathy, however, is his attitude towards Jessica:

   'I would my daughter were dead at my foot, and the jewels in her ear!
   would she were hearsed at my foot, and the ducats in her coffin!'

These are hardly the remarks of an affectionate father! Shylock has been so corrupted that his possessions are of more value to him than his only daughter.

Shylock's Humanity

(1) Shylock's reply to Salerio's *'what is the use of flesh?'* is an eloquent and pathetic plea for tolerance and fair play in a society which is obviously biased against Jews.

> *'Hath not a Jew*
> *eyes? hath not a Jew hands, organs,*
> *dimensions, senses, affections, passions?'*

Solanio and Salerio embody the prejudice which Shylock suffers: they compare him to the devil and make him the butt of vicious jokes and they never afford him the courtesy of a straight answer. Shylock's plea is that of a man who has not been treated as a human being. Is not a Jew as human and vulnerable as anyone else? He asks:

> *'If you prick us, do we not bleed?*
> *if you tickle us, do we not laugh? if you poison*
> *us, do we not die?'*

There is an extent therefore to which Shylock has been driven towards the barbarism he is contemplating: ill-treated people will react at some stage.

> *'The villainy you*
> *teach me I will execute, and it shall go hard but I will*
> *better the instruction.'*

(2) There is real tenderness and genuine emotion in Shylock's reaction to Jessica's mindless disposal of a treasured personal possession:

> *'it was my*
> *turquoise; I had it of Leah when I was a bachelor:*
> *I would not have given it for a wilderness of monkeys.'*

The tragic potential of these words is that Shylock for once values something for its sentimental rather than its financial value and we realise that after all here is a man and not a monster.

Pathos, that quality that raises pity, is the essence of good drama and while we are revolted at Shylock's lust for revenge and his corrupted sense of values, and while we laugh at his misfortunes, we cannot but feel a pang of sympathy for the reviled outsider who is taunted and jeered in the streets and who is betrayed in the most telling manner by the person closest to him.

Scene II

Belmont. A room in Portia's house.
Enter Bassanio, Portia, Gratiano, Nerissa, and Servants

Portia

I pray you, tarry,[1] pause a day or two
Before you hazard; for, in choosing wrong,
I lose your company: therefore, forbear[2] awhile.
There's something tells me (but it is not love)
I would not lose you; and you know yourself,
Hate counsels[3] not in such a quality.
But lest you should not understand me well—
And yet a maiden hath no tongue but thought—
I would detain you here some month or two
Before you venture[4] for me. I could teach you   10
How to choose right, but then I am forsworn;[5]
So will I never be: so may you miss me—
But if you do, you'll make me wish a sin,
That I had been forsworn. Beshrew[6] your eyes,
They have o'erlook'd[7] me and divided me:
One half of me is yours, the other half yours—
Mine own, I would say; but if mine, then yours,
And so all yours. O these naughty times
Put bars between the owners and their rights;
And so, though yours, not yours. Prove it so,   20
Let fortune go to hell for it, not I.
I speak too long; but 'tis to peise[8] the time,
To eke[9] it and to draw it out in length,
To stay[10] you from election.

Bassanio

       Let me choose;
For as I am, I live upon the rack.[11]

Portia

Upon the rack, Bassanio! then confess
What treason there is mingled with your love.

Bassanio

None but that ugly treason of mistrust,
Which makes me fear th' enjoying of my love:
There may as well be amity[12] and life   30
'Tween snow and fire, as treason and my love.

Portia

Ay, but I fear you speak upon the rack,
Where men enforced do speak anything.

[1] wait
[2] be patient
[3] advises
[4] gamble
[5] I would have broken an oath
[6] shame on
[7] entranced
[8] hold back
[9] lengthen
[10] hold
[11] an instrument of torture
[12] friendship

Bassanio

Promise me life, and I'll confess the truth.

Portia

Well, then, confess, and live.

Bassanio

    'Confess and love'

Had been the very sum of my confession:

O happy torment, when my torturer

Doth teach me answers for deliverance![13]

But let me to my fortune and the caskets.

Portia

Away then! I am lock'd in one of them;   40

If you do love me, you will find me out.

Nerissa and the rest, stand all aloof.[14]

Let music sound while he doth make his choice;

Then, if he lose, he makes a swan-like end,[15]

Fading in music: that the comparison

May stand more proper, my eye shall be the stream

And watery death-bed for him. He may win;

And what is music then? then music is

Even as the flourish when true subjects bow

To a new-crowned monarch: such it is   50

As are those dulcet[16] sounds in break of day

That creep into the dreaming bridegroom's ear,

And summon him to marriage. Now he goes,

With no less presence,[17] but with much more love,

Than young Alcides[18], when he did redeem[19]

The virgin tribute[20] paid by howling Troy

To the sea-monster: I stand for sacrifice;

The rest aloof are the Dardanian[21] wives,

With bleared[22] visages[23] come forth to view

The issue[24] of th' exploit. Go, Hercules!   60

Live thou, I live: with much, much more dismay

I view the fight than thou mak'st the fray.

[A Song, whilst Bassanio comments on the caskets to himself

    Tell me where is fancy[25] bred,

    Or in the heart or in the head?

    How begot, how nourished?

    Reply, reply.

    It is engend'red in the eyes,

    With gazing fed; and fancy dies

    In the cradle where it lies.

    Let us all ring fancy's knell: 70

[13]that would free me

[14]away

[15]it is said that a swan sings before its death

[16]sweet

[17]dignified appearance
[18]Hercules
[19]save
[20]a virgin who was being sacrificed
[21]Trojan
[22]tear-stained
[23]faces
[24]the outcome

[25]attraction

> *I'll begin it — Ding, dong, bell.*
> *Ding, dong, bell.*

Bassanio

So may the outward shows[26] be least themselves:[27]
The world is still deceiv'd with ornament
In law, what plea so tainted[28] and corrupt
But, being season'd[29] with a gracious voice,
Obscures the show of evil? In religion,
What damned error, but some sober brow[30]
Will bless it and approve it with a text,[31]
Hiding the grossness with fair ornament?   *80*
 There is no vice so simple but assumes
Some mark of virtue on his outward parts.
How many cowards, whose hearts are all as false
As stairs of sand, wear yet upon their chins
The beards of Hercules and frowning Mars,[32]
Who, inward search'd, have livers white as milk,[33]
And these assume but valour's excrement[34]
To render[35] them redoubted.[36] Look on beauty,
And you shall see 'tis purchas'd by the weight;
Which therein works a miracle in nature,   *90*
Making them lightest[37] that wear most of it:
So are those crisped[38] snaky golden locks
Which make such wanton[39] gambols[40] with the wind,
Upon supposed fairness, often known
To be the dowry of a second head,[41]
The skull that bred them in the sepulchre.[42]
Thus ornament is but the guiled[43] shore
To a most dangerous sea, the beauteous scarf
Veiling an Indian[44] beauty; in a word,
The seeming truth which cunning times put on   *100*
To entrap the wisest. Therefore, thou gaudy gold,
Hard food for Midas,[45] I will none of thee;
Nor none of thee, thou pale and common drudge[46]
'Tween man and man: but thou, thou meagre[47] lead,
Which rather threaten'st than dost promise aught,
Thy paleness moves me more than eloquence,
And here choose I: joy be the consequence!

Portia

[Aside] How all the other passions fleet to air,
As doubtful thoughts, and rash-embrac'd despair,
And shuddering fear, and green-eyed jealousy.   *110*
O love be moderate, allay[48] thy ecstasy,
In measure rein thy joy, scant[49] this excess,

[26]appearances
[27]not what they seem

[28]flawed
[29]given a pleasant taste

[30]a pious-looking person
[31]a quotation from the Bible

[32]the classical god of war
[33]are cowards
[34]the outward signs of courage
[35]make
[36]feared

[37]lightest in character, i.e. most immoral
[38]curled
[39]playful
[40]frolics
[41]i.e. a wig
[42]tomb
[43]treacherous
[44]dark skin was unattractive to the Elizabethans

[45]In Greek mythology everything that Midas touched turned to gold – including his food
[46]unskilled worker
[47]poor

[48]moderate
[49]reduce

I feel too much thy blessing; make it less,
For fear I surfeit!

Bassanio

        What find I here?

               [He opens the leaden casket

50likeness
51almost divine painter
52fixed on
53eyeballs
54parted
55barrier
56separate
57i.e. her lips

Fair Portia's counterfeit![50] What demi-god[51]
Hath come so near creation? Move these eyes?
Or whether, riding[52] on the balls[53] of mine,
Seem they in motion? Here are sever'd[54] lips,
Parted with sugar breath; so sweet a bar[55]
Should sunder[56] such sweet friends.[57] Here in
     her hairs   120
The painter plays the spider, and hath woven
A gold mesh t' entrap the hearts of men
Faster than gnats in cobwebs: but her eyes!
How could he see to do them? having made one,
Methinks it should have power to steal both his
And leave itself unfurnish'd: yet look how far
The substance of my praise doth wrong this shadow
In underprizing it, so far this shadow

58Portia herself

59container

Doth limp behind the substance.[58] Here's the scroll,
The continent[59] and summary of my fortune.   130
    You that choose not by the view,
    Chance as fair, and choose as true!
    Since this fortune falls to you,
    Be content and seek no new.
    If you be well pleas'd with this
    And hold your fortune for your bliss,
    Turn you where your lady is
    And claim her with a loving kiss.
A gentle scroll. Fair lady, by your leave;

               [Kissing her

                140
I came by note, to give and to receive.
Like one of two contending in a prize,
That thinks he hath done well in people's eyes,
Hearing applause and universal shout,
Giddy in spirit, still gazing in a doubt
Whether those peals of praise be his or no;
So, thrice-fair lady, stand I, even so,
As doubtful whether what I see be true,
Until confirm'd, sign'd, ratified by you.

Portia

You see me, Lord Bassanio, where I stand,
Such as I am: though for myself alone   150

I would not be ambitious in my wish,
To wish myself much better; yet, for you,
I would be trebled twenty times myself;
A thousand times more fair, ten thousand
        times more rich;
That only to stand high in your account,[60]
I might in virtues, beauties, livings,[61] friends,
Exceed account: but the full sum of me
Is sum of something, which, to term in gross,
Is an unlesson'd girl, unschool'd, unpractis'd;
Happy in this, she is not yet so old   160
But she may learn; happier than this,
She is not bred so dull but she can learn;
Happiest of all, is that her gentle spirit
Commits itself to yours to be directed
As from her lord, her governor, her king.
Myself and what is mine, to you and yours
Is now converted: but now I was the lord
Of this fair mansion, master of my servants,
Queen o'er myself; and even now, but now,
This house, these servants, and this same self   170
Are yours, my lord's. I give them with this ring;
Which when you part from, lose, or give away,
Let it presage[62] the ruin of your love,
And be my vantage[63] to exclaim[64] on you.

Handwritten margin note: Portia gives everything she has to Bassanio

Handwritten margin note: If he loses the ring he doesn't love her

[60]estimation
[61]possessions

[62]predict
[63]opportunity
[64]speak out against

Bassanio

Madam, you have bereft[65] me of all words,
Only my blood speaks to you in my veins;
And there is such confusion in my powers, As, after some oration
fairly spoke
By a beloved prince, there doth appear
Among the buzzing pleased multitude;
Where every something, being blent together,
Turns to a wild of nothing, save of joy,
Express'd, and not express'd. But when this ring
Parts from this finger, then parts life from hence:
O then be bold to say Bassanio's dead.

[65]deprived

Handwritten margin note: He won't lose the ring   180

Nerissa

My lord and lady, it is now our time,
That have stood by and seen our wishes prosper,
To cry, good joy. Good joy, my lord and lady!

Gratiano

My Lord Bassanio, and my gentle lady,
I wish you all the joy that you can wish;   190

For I am sure you can wish none from me.
And when your honours mean to solemnize
The bargain of your faith, I do beseech you,
Even at that time I may be married too.

I'm happy for you. Can I get married at the same time.

Bassanio

With all my heart, so thou canst get a wife.

Gratiano

I thank your lordship, you have got me one.
My eyes, my lord, can look as swift as yours:
You saw the mistress, I beheld the maid;
You lov'd, I lov'd: for intermission[66]
No more pertains to me, my lord, than you.
Your fortune stood[67] upon the caskets there,   200
And so did mine too, as the matter falls;[68]
For wooing here until I sweat again,
And swearing till my very roof was dry
With oaths of love, at last (if promise last)
I got a promise of this fair one here
To have her love, provided that your fortune
Achiev'd her mistress.

Gratanio's sucess depends on Bassanio's

Portia

     Is this true, Nerissa?

Nerissa

Madam, it is, so you stand pleas'd withal.

Bassanio

And do you, Gratiano, mean good faith?   210

Gratiano

Yes, faith, my lord.

Bassanio

Our feast shall be much honour'd in your marriage.   *Ok!*

Gratiano

We'll play[69] with them the first boy for a thousand ducats.

Nerissa

What, and stake[70] down?

Gratiano

No, we shall ne'er win at that sport and stake down!
But who comes here! Lorenzo and his infidel![71]
What! and my old Venetian friend, Salerio?

    Enter Lorenzo, Jessica, and Salerio

Bassanio

Lorenzo, and Salerio, welcome hither,
If that the youth[72] of my new interest[73] here

[66]a break

[67]depended
[68]as it so happens

[69]compete

[70]a wager, or a pole or post (lewd joke)

[71]one who lacks the true faith, i.e. Jessica

[72]newness
[73]claim

94

Have power to bid you welcome. By your leave,   *220*
I bid my very[74] friends and countrymen,   [74]true
Sweet Portia, welcome.

Portia

     So do I, my lord:
They are entirely welcome.

Lorenzo

I thank your honour. For my part, my lord,
My purpose[75] was not to have seen you here,   [75]intention
But meeting with Salerio by the way,
He did entreat me, past all saying nay,
To come with him along.

Salanio came along

Salerio

     I did, my lord,
And I have reason for it. Signior Antonio
Commends him[76] to you.   *[Gives Bassanio a letter*   [76]sends his kindest regards

Bassanio

     Ere I hope his letter,
I pray you, tell me how my good friend doth.

How is Antonio?

Salerio

Not sick, my lord, unless it be in mind;
Nor well, unless in mind: his letter there
Will show you his estate.[77]   [77]condition

               [Bassanio opens the letter

Gratiano

Nerissa, cheer yond stranger; bid her welcome.
Your hand, Salerio. What's the news from Venice?
How doth that royal merchant, good Antonio?
I know he will be glad of our success;
We are the Jasons,[78] we have won the fleece.   [78]see note 62 Act 1, Scene I

Tells Nerissa to welcome Jessica.

Salerio

I would you had won the fleece that he hath lost.   *240*

Portia

There are some shrewd[79] contents in yond same   [79]evil
     paper,
That steals the colour from Bassanio's cheek:
Some dear friend dead, else nothing in the world
Could turn so much the constitution[80]   [80]temperment, composure
Of any constant[81] man. What, worse and worse!   [81]well-balanced
With leave, Bassanio; I am half yourself,
And I must freely have the half of anything
That this same paper brings you.

Bassanio is upset by the letter.

Bassanio

O sweet Portia!
Here are a few of the unpleasant'st words
That ever blotted paper. Gentle lady,   *250*
When I did first impart my love to you,
I freely told you all the wealth I had
Ran in my veins — I was a gentleman—
And then I told you true: and yet, dear lady,
Rating⁸² myself at nothing, you shall see
How much I was a braggart.⁸³ When I told you
My state⁸⁴ was nothing, I should then have told you
That I was worse than nothing; for, indeed,
I have engag'd myself⁸⁵ to a dear friend,
Engag'd my friend to his mere⁸⁶ enemy,   *260*
To feed my means.⁸⁷ Here is a letter, lady;
The paper as⁸⁸ the body of my friend,
And every word in it a gaping wound,
Issuing life-blood. But is it true, Salerio?
Hath all his ventures fail'd? What, not one hit?
From Tripolis, from Mexico, and England,
From Lisbon, Barbary, and India?
And not one vessel 'scape the dreadful touch
Of merchant-marring⁸⁹ rocks?

Salerio

Not one, my lord.
Besides, it should appear, that if he had   *270*
The present money to discharge⁹⁰ the Jew,
He would not take it. Never did I know
A creature, that did bear the shape of man,
So keen and greedy to confound⁹¹ a man
He plies⁹² the duke at morning and at night,
And doth impeach⁹³ the freedom of the state,
If they deny him justice: twenty merchants,
The duke himself, and the magnificoes⁹⁴
Of greatest port,⁹⁵ have all persuaded with him;
But none can drive him from the envious plea⁹⁶   *280*
Of forfeiture, of justice, and his bond.

Jessica

When I was with him, I have heard him swear
To Tubal and to Chus, his countrymen,
That he would rather have Antonio's flesh
Than twenty times the value of the sum
That he did owe him; and I know, my lord,
If law, authority, and power deny not,
It will go hard with poor Antonio.

---

⁸²valuing
⁸³boastful person

⁸⁴fortune

⁸⁵pledged myself
⁸⁶absolute
⁸⁷to provide me with the
   money I needed
⁸⁸like

⁸⁹ruining

⁹⁰ready money to pay

⁹¹ruin
⁹²pesters

⁹³call into question

⁹⁴nobles
⁹⁵importance
⁹⁶spiteful demand

He didn't say he was in debt.

All the ships were wrecked.

Shylock won't let anyone else pay it back

The money doesn't matter he wants revenge on Antonio.

Portia

Is it your dear friend that is thus in trouble?

Bassanio

The dearest friend to me, the kindest man,   290
The best-condition'd[97] and unwearied spirit
In doing courtesies,[98] and one in whom
The ancient Roman honour more appears
Than any that draws breath in Italy.

> [97]best-natured
> [98]acts of kindness

My Best friend

Portia

What sum owes he the Jew?

Bassanio

For me, three thousand ducats.

Portia

       What, no more?
Pay him six thousand, and deface[99] the bond;
Double six thousand, and then treble that,
Before a friend of this description
Shall lose a hair through Bassanio's fault.   300
First go with me to church and call me wife,
And then away to Venice to your friend;
For never shall you lie by Portia's side
With an unquiet soul. You shall have gold
To pay the petty debt twenty times over:
When it is paid, bring your true friend along.
My maid Nerissa and myself meantime
Will live as maids and widows. Come, away!
For you shall hence[100] upon your wedding-day.
Bid your friends welcome, show a merry cheer: 310
Since you are dear bought, I will love you dear.
But let me hear the letter of your friend.

> [99]destroy, i.e. cancel

> [100]go away from here

Before Bassanio goes back, he has to marry her

Bassanio

*"Sweet Bassanio, my ships have all
miscarried, my creditors grow cruel, my estate is
very-low, my bond to the Jew is forfeit; and since,
in paying it, it is impossible I should live, all
debts are cleared between you and I, if I might but
see you at my death. Notwithstanding, use your
pleasure:[101] if your love do not persuade you to come,
let not my letter."*   320

> [101]nevertheless do as you
> please

He's going to die.

Portia

O love, dispatch[102] all business, and be gone!

> [102]hurry up with

Just Go!

Bassanio

Since I have your good leave to go away,
I will make haste; but, till I come again,
No bed shall e'er be guilty of my stay,
Nor rest be interposer 'twixt us twain.[103]

I wont rest until this is fixed

[Exeunt

[103] rest shall not come
between us two

Summary

Bassanio's Choice

Portia has fallen in love with Bassanio and wants to delay his choice at the caskets in case he chooses incorrectly. She is tempted to show Bassanio the casket that contains her picture but she has given her word and resists the temptation.

Bassanio is impatient, however, and cannot endure the torture of suspense. Portia tells him that true love should direct his choice and orders background music as he prepares to choose. She can hardly bear to watch.

Like Morocco and Arragon before him, Bassanio ponders the caskets. The song in the background is about things that appeal to the eyes and from this he takes his cue. He is suspicious of external appearances from the outset because in law and religion, in military honour and physical beauty, it can conceal inner corruption and has trapped the wisest of men. He consequently rejects the golden casket. He rejects the silver casket too because it symbolises money – the medium of barter between men. He opts simply for the lead casket.

Portia can hardly contain her joy. She watches in ecstacy as Bassanio finds her picture in the casket he has opened. He marvels at how life-like the portrait is, even if Portia is so much more beautiful in reality. The scroll in the casket commends him for the values he chose by, and instructs him to claim Portia with a kiss.

Bassanio is dazed with success and asks Portia to confirm that he is not dreaming. She reassures him but is modest in her description of what he has just won. She wishes she were even better and richer for him and offers him a ring to symbolise that she herself and all that is hers now belong to him. Such is Bassanio's joy that he is at a loss for words: he does, however, promise never to part with the ring.

Nerissa and Gratiano are the first to congratulate Portia and Bassanio and they make the surprising request that they too be married on the same wedding day. Their request is granted and as they banter about which of the couples will have the first son, Lorenzo and Jessica enter in the company of Salerio. Salerio is bearing a letter from Antonio to Bassanio.

The news from Antonio is bad. As Bassanio reads the letter he turns so pale that Portia is concerned for him. He explains to Portia his indebtedness to Antonio and asks Salerio to confirm that Antonio has now lost everything. Salerio confirms the news and goes on to explain that Shylock will not be satisfied with anything less than his pound of flesh and that he has initiated legal proceedings towards that end. Jessica is a witness to her father's malicious intentions: she has heard him say that he would rather have Antonio's flesh than twenty times the amount in the bond.

When Portia realises what a friend Antonio has been to Bassanio, she insists that Bassanio put the fate of his friend before everything else. They will marry straight away but the wedding celebrations will be postponed until Bassanio has returned from Venice and all is well. Portia will provide whatever funding it takes to save Antonio.

Portia asks Bassanio to read Antonio's letter aloud. Antonio says that his losses are complete and that he has not long to live. He clears Bassanio of all debts and only requests that Bassanio visit him before death.

When Portia realises the gravity of the situation she dispatches Bassanio to Venice without a moment's further delay.

Scene Analysis

An Important Scene

We have come to what is in many ways the central scene of the play. All the different plots or stories – the casket story, the bond story and the elopement story – are linked together and harmonised in this scene. The casket story reaches its climax and a new plot, the ring plot, is introduced.

Bassanio's choice at the caskets is undoubtedly the highlight of the scene. That we already know which casket contains Portia's picture heightens suspense, and the long speeches from Portia and Bassanio do nothing to relieve the tension.

Good Omens

The omens for Bassanio are good, however. The scene takes place in an atmosphere of love which contrasts with the two previous casket scenes, and the language is so poetic as to make it an unsuitable vehicle for failure or disappointment. The best omen for Bassanio is that Portia loves him.

> *'I would not lose you; and you know yourself,*
> *Hate counsels not in such a quality.'*

Portia's love and anxiety are so compelling that she finds it difficult to refrain from telling Bassanio which casket to choose.

> *'I could teach you*
> *How to choose right, but then I am forsworn;'*

A Hint Or Two

If Portia manages to resist her temptation to tell Bassanio, she does, however, give him a slight hint:

> *'If you do love me, you will find me out.'*

The song which she orders to accompany Bassanio's choice helps also. Its lyrics re-echo Portia's hint. *'Fancy'*, it tells us, *'is engend'red in the eyes'* and being therefore but an infatuation,

> *'... dies*
> *In the cradle where it lies.'*

The implication is that gratification of the eyes is mistaken and that genuine love is the real clue. And, in case Bassanio has not got the message, the first three lines of the song rhyme with lead!

Away then! I am lock'd in one of them;
If you do love me, you will find me out.   (Portia, Act 3, Sc II)

Bassanio Gets It Right

From the moment that Bassanio starts to speak, it is evident that he is on the right track:

> *'So may the outwards shows be least themselves:*
> *The world is still deceiv'd with ornament...'*

Bassanio spurns the external attraction of gold and since silver symbolises money he rejects that too. There is but one casket left for him to choose:

'...but thou, thou meagre lead,
Which rather threaten'st than dost promise aught,
Thy paleness moves me more than eloquence,
And here choose I:'

Love's Victory

In choosing lead, Bassanio reflects a belief in ideal love which spurns superficial appearances for the genuine worth which is concealed. The scroll in the lead casket vindicates his choice:

'You that choose not by the view,
Chance as fair, and choose as true!'

It repeats what the scroll in the gold casket told Morocco:

'All that glisters is not gold;'

and what Arragon learned from his choice of silver:

'Some there be that shadows kiss:
Such have but a shadow's bliss.'

Love has enabled Bassanio to judge rightly where Morocco and Arragon failed. It has steered him clear of Morocco's rational eloquence and Arragon's self-seeking pride.

What find I here?
Fair Portia's counterfeit! What demi-god
Hath come so near creation?   (Bassanio, Act 3, Sc II)

Shakespeare's Great Theme

And so as the casket story comes to an end, two of the play's great themes – the contrast between appearance and reality, and the supremacy of love, dovetail into one. It is Shakespeare's great theme that the wealth and sensory beauty which gold and silver symbolise are but transitory: real success and real value are found only in the things of the heart. When it came to the crunch, Bassanio's heart was in the right place.

Three Kinds Of Love

Bassanio's ideal love for Portia is not the only kind of love represented in this scene. Gratiano's love for Nerissa is less rapturous and idyllic, more physical and less spiritual. It is something which has involed him in:

> '...wooing here until I sweat again,
> And swearing till my very roof was dry
> With oaths of love,'

Love as friendship is also represented in the relationship of Bassanio and Antonio. Bassanio refers to Antonio as 'the dearest friend to me'. For the Elizabethans, friendship was as precious and important as love. Here it compels Bassanio to abandon his new-found bliss and return to a vicious world to save a friend.

Venice has intruded upon Belmont and the secure world of love has its romantic atmosphere shattered by the grim news of Antonio's impending death.

Characters

PORTIA

The Portia who was so graceful under pressure in the two previous casket scenes finds it very difficult to maintain her composure here. The cool, witty woman has been made vulnerable by love:

> 'Beshrew your eyes,
> They have o'erlook'd me and divided me:'

Love tempts Portia to wear her heart on her sleeve but her father's will demands that she conceal her feelings. She tries to steer a middle course between the conflicting demands but the result is confused and incoherent:

> 'One half of me is yours, the other half yours—
> Mine own, I would say; but if mine, then yours,'

It is all quite frustrating for her:

> 'O these naughty times
> Put bars between the owners and their rights;'

Bassanio's declaration of his love relieves Portia's anxiety somewhat as is evidenced by the teasing she gives him for the *'torture'* metaphor whereby he declares his love. Her word-play displays that wit, spirit and intelligence which we knew were there. As Bassanio goes to the caskets, however, her tension and anxiety return. The caskets are a device which may prove fatal to her happiness and she may become their sacrificial victim:

> *'I stand for sacrifice;'*

She can hardly bear to watch the proceedings:

> *'...with much, much more dismay*
> *I view the fight than thou that mak'st the fray.'*

As Bassanio chooses the lead casket she has to fight again to control her emotion:

> *'O love be moderate, allay thy ecstasy,*
> *In measure rain thy joy, scant this excess,'*

The speech in which Portia reassures and accepts Bassanio is one of the finest in the play. It is full of humility, acceptance and surrender and expresses the pleasure of giving for love. She wishes she were even better for Bassanio:

> *'I would be trebled twenty times myself;*
> *A thousand times more fair, ten thousand times more rich;'*

Portia's humility is remarkable for a woman who is so endowed that she could:

> *'...entrap the hearts of men*
> *Faster than gnats in cobwebs...'*

She tells us:

> *'...the full sum of me is sum of something, which, to term in gross,*
> *Is an unlesson'd girl, unschool'd, unpractis'd;'*

She surrenders herself and all that is hers to Bassanio:

> *'Myself and what is mine, to you and yours*
> *Is now converted:'*

One of the great signs of love is sensitivity and we notice how quick-eyed Portia is when Bassanio blanches on reading Antonio's letter:

> *'There are some shrewd contents in yond same paper,*
> *That steals the colour from Bassanio's cheek:'*

Her reaction to Antonio's plight is immediate, generous and practical:

> *'First go with me to church and call me wife,*
> *And then away to Venice to your friend;'*

BASSANIO

Bassanio is an impatient lover for whom waiting is pure torture.

> *'Let me choose;'* he demands;
> *'For as I am, I live upon the rack.'*

His wish is granted, but before choosing a casket he delivers one of the finest speeches in the play. The language and images are pure poetry and the words are perceptive and wise. He passes over *'outwards shows'* in favour of the less spectacular, for, as he says:

> *'...ornament is but the guiled shore*
> *To a most dangerous sea;'*

And, as we have seen, his values are vindicated.

Bassanio's speech does much to banish the unfavourable impression which he made on us in the opening scenes. His choice of lead in particular diminishes that mercenary aspect of a character who set out to become a rich man through marriage. There is an extent perhaps to which Bassanio has been refined by love.

The Bassanio we meet in this scene is genuinely in love with Portia and he is frank and humble in his suit. He enters to no fanfare and even if Portia sees him as having *'... no less presence ... Than young Alcides,'* he spends no time in praising himself. Unlike Morocco and Arragon, Bassanio makes no pretences whatsover:

> *'When I told you*
> *My state was nothing, I should then have told you*
> *That I was worse than nothing;'*

Bassanio is circumspect also in his new role in Belmont. Though Portia, Lorenzo and Salerio will greet him in quick succession as *'my lord'*, he does not take lightly upon himself the role of welcoming friends to Belmont. To Lorenzo and Salerio he says:

> *'welcome hither,*
> *If that the youth of my new interest here*
> *Have power to bid you welcome.'*

Bassanio's most endearing quality, however, is his loyalty to Antonio. He is visibly distraught at Antonio's letter and is willing to abandon the haven of his new-found bliss to save a friend in need.

SHYLOCK

Though Shylock is not present in this scene, we learn a lot about him. If there was some scope for sympathy for him in the previous scene, there is none here. Shylock's villainy reigns supreme. Salerio is scathing in his criticism of *'the Jew'*:

> *'Never did I know*
> *A creature, that did bear the shape of man,*
> *So keen and greedy to confound a man...'*

The energy and vigour whereby Shylock pursues his object, which was evident at the end of the previous scene, is reported again here:

> *'He plies the duke at morning and at night,*
> *And doth impeach the freedom of the state,*
> *If they deny him justice:'*

There is no talking to him now: he is unchangeable, unreasonable and uncompromising:

> *'...none can drive him from the envious plea*
> *Of forfeiture, of justice, and his bond.'*

The quality most evident in Shylock now is his vindictiveness: his own daughter alleges that his passion for revenge outweighs his avarice:

> *'...he would rather have Antonio's flesh*
> *Than twenty times the value of the sum*
> *That he did owe him;'*

The significance of Jessica's revelation is that Shylock had made up his mind to kill Antonio long before her elopement with Lorenzo and that he has made speeches at home to that effect.

Bad Omens For Shylock

Bassanio's success at Belmont bodes ill for Shylock, however. The victory of considerations of the heart over financial and materialistic considerations augurs poorly for the Midas-figure of the play and his corrupted sense of values.

Bassanio's victory also brings Portia on to Antonio's side and means that Shylock has a new adversary who has intelligence, wit and spirit, backed up with very considerable means.

> *'...twenty merchants,*
> *The duke himself, and the magnificoes*
> *of greatest port,'*

are already taking a contrary view to Shylock and now Belmont is against him too.

With Belmont and Venice against him, what chance will Shylock have? Is it not inevitable that the Christian world will reassert itself and in so doing destroy him?

ANTONIO

Everything has gone wrong for Antonio, and his letter to Bassanio says it all:

> '...my ships have all
> miscarried, my creditors grow cruel, my estate is
> very-low, my bond to the Jew is forfeit; and ...
> in paying it, it is impossible I should live...'

Antonio's merchant fleet has been completely wiped out:

> '...not one vessel 'scape the dreadful touch
> Of merchant-marring rocks?'

Bassanio gives Portia a glowing description of his friend who is in trouble:

> 'The dearest friend to me, the kindest man,
> The best-condition'd and unwearied spirit
> In doing courtesies,'

Antonio has displayed supreme loyalty to friends and to country. He has been:

> 'one in whom
> The ancient Roman honour more appears
> Than any that draws breath in Italy.'

These words have the unmistakeable ring of an epitaph and if the last line indicates Antonio's continued existence, there is the implication that he may not draw breath for very much longer.

His letter is pathetic in the extreme and noticeable for the way it avoids apportioning blame. In clearing Bassanio of all debts, Antonio reveals a noble mind, and his last request that he might see Bassanio before dying reminds us of Solanio's remark in Act 2, Scene IX:

> 'I think he only loves the world for him.'

Scene III

Venice. A street
Enter Shylock, Solanio, Antonio, and Gaoler

Shylock

Gaoler, look to him: tell not me of mercy; *[handwritten: Why would I have mercy on him?]*
This is the fool that lent out money gratis:[1]   [1]free of interest
Gaoler, look to him.

Antonio

       Hear me yet, good Shylock. *[handwritten: Let me talk to you.]*

Shylock

I'll have my bond; speak not against my bond:
I have sworn an oath that I will have my bond. *[handwritten: If you insult me this is what happens]*
Thou call'dst me dog before thou hadst a cause,
But, since I am a dog, beware my fangs:
The duke shall grant me justice. I do wonder,
Thou naughty[2] gaoler, that thou are so fond[3]   [2]good-for-nothing
To come abroad[4] with him at his request.   10   [3]foolish
                                                                    [4]out of prison

Antonio

I pray thee, hear me speak.

Shylock

I'll have my bond; I will not hear thee speak: *[handwritten: No.]*
I'll have my bond, and therefore speak no more.
I'll not be made a soft and dull-eyed fool,
To shake the head, relent, and sigh, and yield
To Christian intercessors.[5] Follow not;   [5]peacemakers
I'll have no speaking; I will have my bond.   [Exit

Solanio

It is the most impenetrable cur[6] *[handwritten: He's an animal]*   [6]hard-hearted dog
That ever kept with[7] men.   [7]lived with

Antonio

    Let him alone:
I'll follow him no more with bootless[8] prayers. *[handwritten: I had it coming to me.]*
He seeks my life; his reason well I know.   20   [8]useless
I oft deliver'd from his forfeitures[9]
Many that have at times made moan[10] to me;   [9]rescued from his penalties
Therefore he hates me.   [10]complained

Solanio

    I am sure the duke
Will never grant this forfeiture to hold.

Antonio

[11]commercial privileges
[12]foreigners
[13]call into question

The duke cannot deny the course of law:
For the commodity[11] that strangers[12] have
With us in Venice, if it be denied,
Will much impeach[13] the justice of the state,
Since that the trade and profit of the city
Consisteth of all nations. Therefore, go:

[14]wasted

These griefs and losses have so bated[14] me,
That I shall hardly spare a pound of flesh
Tomorrow to my bloody creditor.
Well, gaoler, on. Pray God, Bassanio come
To see me pay his debt, and then I care not!

30

*No choice.
Reputation of Venice at stake.*

[Exeunt

Summary

Antonio Meets Shylock

Antonio has been placed under arrest but has persuaded his gaoler to take him out of prison so that he can meet Shylock and plead for mercy. Shylock warns the gaoler to guard the prisoner carefully and taunts Antonio for lending money free of interest.

Shylock is impervious to Antonio's attempts to reason with him. He refuses to listen and reiterates repeatedly that he will have his bond. He will act like the dog Antonio was wont to call him: he will have justice as he sees it and will not be softened by any amount of pleading. Furthermore, he does not approve of the flimsy pretext on which the prisoner has been taken out from behind bars.

Solanio, who is present at the meeting, launches into an attack on Shylock, calling him a hard-hearted dog. Antonio asks him to desist, however: he knows that since in the past he has saved many debtors from ruin at the hands of Shylock, he cannot expect any favours from Shylock now.

Solanio tries to console Antonio with the sentiment that the duke would never allow the terms of the bond to be enforced. But Antonio knows that the duke's hands are tied: Venice has to protect its commerical and legal reputation and strict justice must be seen to be done. Antonio has lost so much weight with worry that he doubts if there will be enough of him for his bloodthirsty creditor. He has lost hope and all he cares about now is that his friend Bassanio be with him at the end.

Scene Analysis

The picture of a resigned Antonio and a doggedly ferocious Shylock given in the previous scene is suddenly animated here as the defendant and prosecutor walk on stage before us.

As Bassanio leaves Belmont, events in Venice are moving towards a climax. The three months of the bond have elapsed and Antonio is under arrest: Shylock is impervious to reasoning and it appears that the full rigour of Venetian law must be brought to bear on Antonio. Venice depends on its international reputation for honouring contracts and confidence in Venetian justice would be shaken if the law was bent to help a Venetian.

> 'The duke cannot deny the course of law:
> For the commodity that strangers have
> With us in Venice, if it be denied,
> Will much impeach the justice of the state,
> Since that the trade and profit of the city
> Consisteth of all nations.'

The bond plot appears to be heading inevitably towards a bloody culmination.

He seeks my life; his reasons well I know. (Antonio, Act 3, Sc III)

Characters

Another Look At The Prosecutor And The Defendant

SHYLOCK

There can no longer be any doubt about the reality and ferocity of the threat to Antonio which Shylock embodies. Shylock will not listen to a word of reason:

> '– tell me not of mercy...'
> 'I will not hear thee speak:'

As far as Shylock is concerned, any listening to Antonio's pleas for mercy would show weakness.

> 'I'll not be made a soft and dull-eyed fool,
> To shake the head, relent, and sigh, and yield
> To Christian intercessors.'

Shylock has convinced himself that his hardness of heart is justified:

> 'Thou call'dst me dog before thou hadst a cause,
> But, since I am a dog, beware my fangs:'

When Solanio calls Shylock an 'impenetrable cur', however, he ironically and unwittingly illustrates Shylock's complaint and substantiates his motives. Antonio understands Shylock's motives only too well:

> 'He seeks my life; his reason well I know.
> I oft deliver'd from his forfeitures
> Many that have at times made moan to me;
> Therefore he hates me.'

Shylock's compulsive repetition of 'I'll have my bond' shows that he is possessed now by a single thought. He has hardened his heart and closed his ears and primed himself as a destructive homing-device which, it appears, can no longer be turned off.

ANTONIO

It is surprising, to say the least of it, to find Antonio addressing his prosecutor as 'good Shylock'. He has evidently swallowed his pride as he humbles himself before his old enemy.

> 'I pray thee, hear me speak.'

Shylock, for his part, turns humility into humiliation:

> 'This is the fool that lent out money gratis.'

Yet it is Antonio that wins our sympathy – not so much because he is humbled, as for the growth in his understanding and his mellowing towards Shylock.

> '...his reason well I know.'

Antonio's kindness and generosity still contrast sharply with Shylock's vindictiveness and spite. Antonio does not win our esteem however, because of the passive and fatalistic manner in which he accepts his situation:

> 'Let him alone:
> I'll follow him no more with bootless prayers.'

His words are full of self-pity:

> 'These griefs and losses have so bated me,
> That I shall hardly spare a pound of flesh
> Tomorrow to my bloody creditor.'

Antonio goes into the court with our sympathy, but he is a defeated man who lacks the gumption and self-assertion to defend himself. If he is to survive, someone else will have to do it for him.

Scene IV

Belmont. A room in Portia's house
Enter Portia, Nerissa, Lorenzo, Jessica, and Balthazar

Lorenzo

Madam, although I speak it in your presence,
You have a noble and a true conceit[1]
Of god-like amity;[2] which appears most strongly
In bearing thus the absence of your lord.
But if you knew to whom you show this honour,
How true a gentleman you send relief,
How dear a lover of my lord your husband,
I know you would be prouder of the work
Than customary bounty[3] can enforce you.

Portia

I never did repent for doing good,   *10*
Nor shall not now: for in companions

[1] understanding
[2] friendship

[3] your usual goodness

Greeting Portia and praising Antonio

That do converse and waste[4] the time together,
Whose souls do bear an equal yoke of love[5],
There must be needs[6] a like[7] proportion
Of lineaments,[8] of manners, and of spirit;
Which makes me think that this Antonio,
Being the bosom lover[9] of my lord,
Must needs be like my lord. If it be so,
How little is the cost I have bestow'd
In purchasing the semblance[10] of my soul
From out the state of hellish cruelty!
This comes too near the praising of myself;
Therefore, no more of it: hear other things.
Lorenzo, I commit into your hands
The husbandry[11] and manage[12] of my house
Until my lord's return: for mine own part,
I have toward heaven breath'd a secret vow
To live in prayer and contemplation,
Only attended by Nerissa here,
Until her husband and my lord's return.
There is a monastery two miles off,
And there we will abide. I do desire you
Not to deny this imposition,[13]
The which my love and some necessity
Now lays upon you.

Lorenzo

　　Madam, with all my heart:
I shall obey you in all fair commands.

Portia

My people do already know my mind,
And will acknowledge you and Jessica
In place of Lord Bassanio and myself
So fare you well till we shall meet again.   40

Lorenzo

Fair thoughts and happy hours attend on you!

Jessica

I wish your ladyship all heart's content.

Portia

I thank you for your wish, and am well pleas'd
To wish it back on you: fare you well, Jessica.
                    [Exeunt Jessica and Lorenzo

Now, Balthazar,
As I have ever found thee honest-true,

Sidenotes:
[4] spend
[5] are well matched in friendship
[6] there must be of necessity
[7] a similar
[8] characteristics
[9] intimate friend
[10] likeness
[11] care
[12] management
[13] task that I impose

Handwritten margin notes:
Antonio must be a good man. She is happy to help him (near line 20)
She and Nerissa are leaving. (near line 30)

So let me find thee still. Take this same letter,
And use thou all th'endeavour of a man
In speed to Padua: see thou render[14] this

Go send a letter

[14]give

Into my cousin's hand, Doctor Bellario;   50
And look what notes and garments he doth give thee,

get stuff and melt them

Bring them, I pray thee, with imagin'd speed[15]
Unto the traject,[16] to the common ferry

[15]as quickly as possible
[16]crossing place

Which trades to Venice. Waste no time in words,
But get thee gone: I shall be there before thee.

Balthazar

Madam, I go with all convenient[17] speed.   [Exit   [17]appropriate

Portia

Come on, Nerissa: I have work in hand
That you yet know not of: we'll see our husbands
Before they think of us.

Nerissa

        Shall they see us?

Portia

They shall, Nerissa; but in such a habit[18]   60   [18]clothes
That they shall think we are accomplished
With that we lack. I'll hold thee any wager,
When we are both accoutered[19] like young men,   [19]dressed up

They'll dress up like men

I'll prove the prettier fellow of the two,
And wear my dagger with the braver grace,
And speak between the change of man and boy[20]   [20]like a boy whose voice is
With a reed[21] voice, and turn two mincing[22] steps   breaking
Into a manly stride, and speak of frays   [21]shrill
Like a fine bragging youth, and tell quaint[23] lies,   [22]dainty
How honourable ladies sought my love,   70   [23]cleverly contrived
Which I denying, they fell sick and died —
I could not do withal;[24] then I'll repent,   [24]I could not do anything
And wish, for all that, that I had not kill'd them.   about it
And twenty of these puny[25] lies I'll tell,   [25]childish
That men shall swear I have discontinu'd school
Above a twelvemonth. I have within my mind
A thousand raw[26] tricks of these bragging jacks,[27]   [26]crude
Which I will practise.   [27]impudent

Nerissa

        Why, shall we turn to men?

Portia

Fie, what a question's that,
If thou wert near a lewd interpreter![28]   80   [28]a person with a dirty mind

²⁹plan

But come: I'll tell thee all my whole device²⁹
When I am in my coach, which stays for us
At the park gate; and therefore haste away,

³⁰travel

For we must measure³⁰ twenty miles today.   *[Exeunt*

I'll explain on the way

Summary

Portia Goes Into Action

Lorenzo compliments Portia for the wonderful manner in which she is taking the absence of Bassanio. He adds that if she knew Antonio she would be very proud of the effort to save him.

Portia rejoins that she never regrets doing a good turn and since Antonio probably resembles Bassanio he is well worth saving. She asks Lorenzo to take over the running of the house until Bassanio's return, saying that she and Nerissa will meanwhile retire to a nearby convent for prayer and contemplation.

The position has been carefully explained to the servants.

As Lorenzo and Jessica depart to take up their new duties, Portia turns to her servant Balthazar and asks him to take the ferry to Padua immediately so that he can procure legal robes and documents from her cousin Dr Bellario. She evidently intends that Nerissa and herself should follow Bassanio and Gratiano to Venice, disguised as men. They will impersonate the dashing mannerisms of brash young men and Portia has plenty of ideas as to how to give a convincing impression.

Nerissa does not know what is going on, but a coach is waiting and Portia will explain everything to her on the way.

Scene Analysis

Scene IV gives us a close-up view of Portia and prepares the way for her appearance in court for the trial scene. It offers some comic relief and the reassurance of ordinary human relationships after the bare-nerved tension and inhuman animosities of the previous scene. Shakespeare perhaps is reminding us that even if Antonio's life hangs in the balance, we are still watching what is after all a comedy.

Much of the humour of the scene arises from the prospect of Portia and Nerissa disguising themselves as men. It is a device that Jessica has already resorted to and the richness of the humour derives from the fact that Portia and Nerissa would with little doubt have been acted by two young boys whose voices had not yet broken. There was always the danger that such voices would break at any moment; that Portia should propose to:

> '...speak between the change of man and boy
> With a reed voice,'

has something of an insurance policy about it.

There is humour too in those aspects of youthful masculinity which Portia highlights. We know that young trade apprentices were common among Shakespeare's audience and there is no doubt that they would have felt themselves 'got at' in some of Portia's remarks about the *'raw tricks of these bragging jacks'*.

When we are both accoutered like young men,
I'll prove the prettier fellow of the two,
And wear my dagger with the braver grace...   *(Portia, Act 3, Sc IV)*

Characters

A Close-Up View Of Portia

Unburdened of the strictures of her father's will, Portia goes into action and her resourcefulness and self-reliance in so doing contrasts sharply with the passive fatalism and lack of self-assertion which we witnessed in Antonio. Portia has a clear, practical grasp of the situation and wastes no time in getting her scheme underway:

> 'Waste no time in words,
> But get thee gone: I shall be there before thee.'

Combined with this self-assured efficiency is a girlish mischieviousness which anticipates with relish the prospect of playing the part of a young man.

> 'I'll hold thee any wager,
> When we are both accoutered like young men,
> I'll prove the prettier fellow of the two,
> And wear my dagger with the braver grace,'

She is not perhaps the 'unlesson'd girl, unschool'd, unpractis'd' that she told Bassanio she was, nor is she totally innocent in the ways of the world:

> 'I have within my mind
> A thousand raw tricks of these bragging jacks.'

Shakespeare is preparing us for the formidable heroine we are soon to encounter.

Scene V

Belmont. Portia's garden.
Enter Launcelot, and Jessica

Launcelot

Yes, truly; for, look you, the sins of the father are to be laid upon[1] the children; therefore, I promise you, I fear you.[2] I was always plain[3] with you, and so now I speak my agitation[4] of the matter: therefore be o' good cheer; for, truly, I think you are damned. There is but one hope in it that can do you any good, and that is but a kind of bastard[5] hope neither.

Jessica

And what hope is that, I pray thee?

Launcelot

Marry, you may partly hope that your father got you not, that you are not the Jew's daughter.

Jessica

That were a kind of bastard hope, indeed: so the sins of my mother should be visited upon me.

[1] revenged upon
[2] I fear for you
[3] honest
[4] he means 'cogitation' or 'thought'

[5] false, illegitimate

Launcelot is worried that Jessica won't get to heaven. 10

Launcelot

Truly then I fear you are damned both by father and
mother: thus when I shun Scylla (your father) I
fall into Charybdis (your mother):[6] well, you are
gone both
ways.

Jessica

I shall be saved by my husband; he hath made me a
Christian.

Launcelot

Truly the more to blame he: we were Christians   20
enow[7] before; e'en as many as could well live one by
another. This making of Christians will raise the
price of hogs: if we grow all to be pork-eaters, we
shall not shortly have a rasher on the coals[8] for money.[9]

Enter Lorenzo

Jessica

I tell my husband, Launcelot, what you say: here he comes.

Lorenzo

I shall grow jealous of you shortly, Launcelot,
if you thus get my wife into corners.

Jessica

Nay, you need not fear us, Lorenzo: Launcelot and I
are out.[10] He tells me flatly there's no mercy for
me in heaven, because I am a Jew's daughter: and he   30
says you are no good member of the commonwealth,
for, in converting Jews to Christians, you raise the
price of pork.

Lorenzo

I shall answer that better to the commonwealth
than you can the getting up of the negro's belly:[11] the
Moor[12] is with child by you, Launcelot.

Launcelot

It is much that the Moor should be more than reason;
but if she be less than an honest[13] woman, she is
indeed more than I took her for.

Lorenzo

How every fool can play upon the word! I think the   40
best grace[14] of wit will shortly turn into silence, and
discourse[15] grow commendable in none only but
parrots. Go in, sirrah: bid them prepare for dinner.

Launcelot

That is done, sir; they have all stomachs[16].

[6] In Greek mythology Scylla and Charybdis were monsters, one taking the form of a rock, the other a whirlpool. They were on either side of the straits of Messina and mariners who escaped one were often caught by the other

[7] enough

[8] cooking on the fire
[9] for any money

[10] have fallen out

[11] getting a negro woman pregnant
[12] Moorish woman

[13] chaste

[14] virtue
[15] talking

[16] appetites

[17] one who snaps up every opportunity to be witty

Lorenzo

Goodly Lord, what a wit-snapper[17] are you! then bid them prepare dinner.

Launcelot

This is done too, sir; only 'cover' is the word.

Lorenzo

Will you cover, then, sir?

Launcelot

[18] Launcelot pretends to confuse 'cover' as in laying a table with 'cover' as in putting on one's hat

[19] taking every opportunity to quibble

Not so, sir, neither; I know my duty.[18]

Lorenzo

Yet more quarrelling with occasion![19] Wilt thou show
the whole wealth of thy wit in an instant? I pray   50
thee, understand a plain man in his plain meaning:
go to thy fellows; bid them cover the table, serve
in the meat, and we will come in to dinner.

Launcelot

[20] as you fancy

For the table, sir, it shall be served in; for the
meat, sir, it shall be covered; for your coming in
to dinner, sir, why, let it be as humours and
conceits shall govern.[20]

They all talk about how wonderful they all are

[Exit

Lorenzo

[21] common sense
[22] applied

O dear discretion[21], how his words are suited![22]
The fool hath planted in his memory
An army of good words, and I do know   60

[23] who occupy better positions
[24] equipped
[25] clever
[26] fail to make sense
[27] how are you?

A many fools, that stand in better place,[23]
Garnish'd[24] like him, that for a tricksy[25] word
Defy the matter.[26] How cheer'st thou,[27] Jessica?
And now, good sweet, say thy opinion;
How dost thou like the Lord Bassanio's wife?

Jessica

[28] beyond words
[29] appropriate

Past all expressing.[28] It is very meet[29]
The Lord Bassanio live an upright life,
For, having such a blessing in his lady,
He finds the joys of heaven here on earth;   70
And if on earth he do not merit it,

[30] it is only reasonable that

In reason[30] he should never come to heaven.
Why, if two gods should play some heavenly match,
And on the wager lay two earthly women,
And Portia one, there must be something else
Pawn'd with the other, for the poor rude world

[31] her equal

Hath not her fellow.[31]

Lorenzo

Even such a husband
Hast thou of me, as she is for a wife.

Jessica

Nay, but ask my opinion too of that.

Lorenzo

I will anon:[32] first, let us go to dinner. 80

[32]soon

Jessica

Nay, let me praise you while I have a stomach.[33]

[33]an appetite, an inclination to praise you

Lorenzo

No, pray thee, let it serve for table-talk;
Then howsome'er[34] thou speak'st, 'mong other things
I shall digest it

[34]however

Jessica

Well, I'll set you forth.[35]

[35]I'll show you up

[*Exeunt*

Summary

In Portia's garden in Belmont, Launcelot Gobbo is teasing Jessica about her Jewish nationality. Her only hope of being saved from damnation, he tells her, is that she prove to be illegitimate. Jessica claims that she has been saved by marrying a Christian, to which Launcelot replies that there are already so many Christians that the price of pigs is rising and that soon a rasher won't be available at any price.

Lorenzo enters and pretends to take offence at Launcelot's intimacy with Jessica. Jessica tells him that there is no need to be jealous for Launcelot and herself are quarrelling. A comic exchange follows in which Lorenzo accuses Launcelot of being responsible for the pregnancy of a Moorish girl. Launcelot, undeterred, persists in his witticisms until Lorenzo grows tired of them and sends him off to see that dinner is prepared.

Alone now with Jessica, Lorenzo laughs at Launcelot's talent in finding different meanings in words to suit his purposes. He asks Jessica what she thinks of Portia: Jessica thinks that Bassanio is blessed in his wife because there is no woman in the world who is Portia's equal.

Lorenzo tells Jessica that she has been as lucky in the man she found as Bassanio was in finding Portia. Jessica has an opinion to offer on that, but dinner is ready and she must keep it for conversation during the meal.

Scene Analysis

Scene V is a brief and inconsequential scene which nevertheless has a number of dramatic functions. Shakespeare gives Portia and Nerissa time to change clothes and creates the impression of time passing so that they can get to Venice by the next scene.

He is, at the same time, giving further scope to the talents of the company's comedian. Two scenes of comic relief in quick succession indicates that Shakespeare is preparing his audience for the harrowing tension and emotion of the long trial scene. Launcelot's clowning and punning induce a calm before the storm of deadly seriousness which is about to follow.

For a modern audience the humour is somewhat tedious and is especially laboured when read from the page. The racial and sexual jokes, moreover, display attitudes towards pregnancy, towards illegitimacy and towards people which are no longer seen as amusing.

Characters

The purpose of this scene is to provide light relief before the tension of the trial scene and little scope is afforded to character development. It does, however, keep **Portia** before our minds through the lavish praise which Jessica bestows upon her. To Jessica, Portia is *'Past all expressing'*. Her qualities are such that:

> *'...The poor rude world*
> *Hath not her fellow.'*

Bassanio has:

> *'...such a blessing in his lady,* (that)
> *He finds the joys of heaven here on earth;'*

We notice also the extent to which **Jessica** has blossomed in Belmont. The enchanted place is obviously more conducive to her nature than the *'hell'* which was her home, and her affection and tenderness towards Lorenzo shows that she has completed her journey from hatred to love.

Launcelot takes up much of the scene with his witticisms. He is the forward *'wit-snapper'* who:

> *'...hath planted in his memory*
> *An army of good words,'*

but whose humour is sometimes hard to take, even for Lorenzo who asks the persistent fool;

> *'Wilt thou show*
> *the whole wealth of thy wit in an instant?'*

This does not prevent **Lorenzo** – the *'plain man'* as he sees himself – from indulging in some wit-snapping of his own as he compares himself to Portia.

> *'Even such a husband*
> *Hast thou of me, as she is for a wife.'*

Act 4

Scene 1

Venice. A Court of Justice

Enter the Duke, the Merchants, Antonio, Bassanio, Gratiano, Salerio and Officers of the Court

Duke

What, is Antonio here?

Antonio

Ready, so please your Grace.

Duke

I am sorry for thee: thou art come to answer
A stony[1] adversary, an inhuman wretch
Uncapable of pity, void[2] and empty
From any dram[3] of mercy.

[1] unfeeling
[2] empty
[3] drop

Sorry for Antonio.

Antonio

    I have heard
Your Grace hath ta'en great pains to qualify[4]
His rigorous course; but since he stands obdurate,[5]
And that no lawful means can carry me
Out of his envy's reach, I do oppose   10
My patience to his fury, and am arm'd[6]
To suffer with a quietness of spirit
The very tyranny and rage of his.

[4] moderate
[5] remains hard-hearted
[6] prepared

Antonio is defeated and has accepted.

Duke

Go one, and call the Jew into the court.

Salerio

He is ready at the door: he comes, my lord.

Enter Shylock

Duke

Make room, and let him stand before our face.
Shylock, the world thinks, and I think so too,
That thou but lead'st this fashion of thy malice[7]
To the last hour of act;[8] and then 'tis thought
Thou'lt show thy mercy and remorse[9] more
    strange[10]   20
Than is thy strange[11] apparent[12] cruelty;
And where thou now exact'st the penalty—
Which is a pound of this poor merchant's flesh—
Thou wilt not only loose the forfeiture,

[7] you are keeping up the appearance of hatred
[8] until the last moment
[9] compassion
[10] wonderful
[11] unnatural
[12] seeming

Hoping Shylock to change his mind at the last minute.

[13]allow him to keep a
portion of the original
sum borrowed

[14]enough

[15]sympathy for

[16]hard hearts

[17]acts

But, touch'd with human gentleness and love,
Forgive a moiety of the principal,[13]
Glancing an eye of pity on his losses,
That have of late so huddled on his back,
Enow[14] to press a royal merchant down,
And pluck commiseration of[15] his state   30
From brassy bosoms[16] and rough hearts of flints,
From stubborn Turks and Tartars, never train'd
To offices[17] of tender courtesy,
We all expect a gentle answer, Jew.

So then everyone will thank Shylock

Shylock

[18]informed

[19]intend to do

[20]fall

[21]rotten

[22]whim

I have possess'd[18] your Grace of what I purpose;[19]
And by our holy Sabbath have I sworn
To have the due and forfeit of my bond:
If you deny it, let the danger light[20]
Upon your charter and your city's freedom.
You'll ask me, why I rather choose to have   40
A weight of carrion[21] flesh than to receive
Three thousand ducats. I'll not answer that,
But say it is my humour.[22] Is it answer'd?
What if my house be troubled with a rat,
And I be pleas'd to give ten thousand ducats
To have it ban'd? What, are you answer'd yet?

Because he hates Antonio

[23]roasted pig's head

[24]drones

[25]prejudice

[26]feelings

Some men there are love not a gaping pig;[23]
Some, that are mad if they behold a cat;
And others, when the bagpipe sings i' the nose,[24]
Cannot contain their urine: for affection,[25]   50
Master of passion,[26] sways it to the mood
Of what it likes, or loathes. Now, for your answer:
As there is no firm reason to be render'd,

[27]tolerate

[28]useful

[29]covered with woollen
cloth

[30]of necessity

Why he cannot abide[27] a gaping pig;
Why he, a harmless necessary[28] cat;
Why he, a woollen[29] bagpipe, but of force[30]
Must yield to such inevitable shame
As to offend, himself being offended;
So can I give no reason, nor I will not

[31]deep-seated

[32]if Shylock gets his pound
of flesh he will lose the
three thousand ducats

[33]course

More than a lodg'd[31] hate and a certain loathing   60
I bear Antonio, that I follow thus
A losing suit[32] against him. Are you answer'd?

Bassanio

This is no answer, thou unfeeling man,
To excuse the current[33] of thy cruelty.

Shylock

I am not bound to please thee with my answers.

Bassanio

Do all men kill the things they do not love?

Shylock

Hates any man the thing he would not kill?

Do you really hate something you wouldn't kill

Bassanio

Every offence is not a hate³⁴ at first.

³⁴a cause for hatred

Shylock

What! wouldst thou have a serpent sting thee twice?

Antonio

I pray you, think³⁵ you question with the Jew: 70

You may as well go stand upon the beach,

And bid the main flood³⁶ bate³⁷ his usual height;

You may as well use question with the wolf,

Why he hath made the ewe bleat for the lamb;

You may as well forbid the mountain pines

To wag their high tops, and to make no noise

When they are fretten³⁸ with the gusts of heaven;

You may as well do anything most hard,

As seek to soften that — than which what's

        harder?—

His Jewish heart: therefore, I do beseech you,   80

Make no more offers, use no farther means;

But with all brief and plain conveniency,³⁹

Let me have judgment, and the Jew his will.

³⁵remember that

³⁶the tide

³⁷reduce

Begging won't work

³⁸fretted, troubled

STOP

³⁹without further ado

Bassanio

For thy three thousand ducats here is six.

Shylock

If every ducat in six thousand ducats

Were in six parts, and every part a ducat,

I would not draw⁴⁰ them. I would have my bond.

⁴⁰take

Duke

How shalt thou hope for mercy, rendering none?

Shylock

What judgment shall I dread, doing no wrong?

You have among you many a purchas'd slave,   90

Which, like your asses and your dogs and mules,

You use in abject⁴¹ and in slavish parts,⁴²

Because you bought them: shall I say to you,

Let them be free, marry them to your heirs?

Why sweat they under burdens? let their beds

Be made as soft as yours, and let their palates

Be season'd with such viands?⁴³ You will answer,

⁴¹low

⁴²tasks

⁴³let their tastes be gratified
  with the same food as
  your own

'The slaves are ours'. So do I answer you:
The pound of flesh which I demand of him,
Is dearly bought; 'tis mine and I will have it.
If you deny me, fie[44] upon your law!   100
There is no force in the decrees of Venice.
I stand for judgment. Answer — shall I have it?

I am entitled to it.

Calling them hypocrites.

44 shame

Duke

Upon my power I may dismiss this court,
Unless Bellario, a learned doctor,
Whom I have sent for to determine this,
Come here today.

Salerio

My lord, here stays without[45]
A messenger with letters from the doctor,
New come from Padua.

45 waits outside

Duke

Bring us the letters: call the messenger.   110

Bassanio

Good cheer, Antonio! What, man, courage yet!
The Jew shall have my flesh, blood, bones, and all,
Ere thou shalt lose for me one drop of blood.

going to stop Shylock

Antonio

I am a tainted[46] wether[47] of the flock,
Meetest[48] for death: the weakest kind of fruit
Drops earliest to the ground; and so let me.
You cannot better be employ'd, Bassanio,
Than to live still, and write mine epitaph. ← *On a gravestone.*

He is ready for death.

46 diseased
47 a ram that has been castrated
48 most suitable

Enter Nerissa, dressed like a lawyer's clerk

Duke

Came you from Padua, from Bellario?

Nerissa

From both, my lord. Bellario greets your Grace.   120
[Presents a letter

Bassanio

Why dost thou whet[49] thy knife so earnestly?

49 sharpen

Shylock

To cut the forfeiture from that bankrupt there.

Gratiano

Not on thy sole, but on thy soul, harsh Jew,

Thou mak'st thy knife keen;[50] but no metal can,
No, not the hangman's axe, bear half the keenness
Of thy sharp envy. Can no prayers pierce thee?

[50]sharp

Your knife will never be as sharp as your envy.

Shylock

No, none that thou hast wit enough to make.

Gratiano

O, be thou damn'd, inexorable[51] dog!
And for thy life[52] let justice be accus'd.
Thou almost mak'st me waver in my faith   130
To hold opinion with Pythagoras,[53]
That souls of animals infuse[54] themselves
Into the trunks[55] of men: thy currish[56] spirit
Govern'd a wolf, who, hang'd[57] for human slaughter,
Even from the gallows did his fell[58] soul fleet,[59]
And whilst thou lay'st in thy unhallow'd dam,[60]
Infus'd itself in thee; for thy desires
Are wolvish, bloody, starv'd and ravenous.

[51]relentless
[52]because of your very existence
[53]a Greek philosopher who believed in the transmigration of souls
[54]pour
[55]bodies
[56]dog-like
[57]was hanged
[58]evil
[59]speed away
[60]unholy mother

A wolf's spirit took over Shylock.

Shylock

Till thou canst rail[61] the seal from off my bond.
Thou but offend'st thy lungs to speak so loud: 140
Repair thy wit, good youth, or it will fall
To cureless[62] ruin. I stand here for law.

[61]scold

[62]incurable

Don't waste your breath.

Duke

This letter from Bellario doth commend
A young and learned doctor to our court.
Where is he?

Nerissa

        He attendeth here hard[63] by,
To know your answer, whether you'll admit him.

[63]near

Duke

With all my heart: some three or four of you
Go give him courteous conduct[64] to this place.

[64]escort

                                        [Exeunt Officers

Meantime, the court shall hear Bellario's letter.
Your Grace shall understand that at the receipt of
your letter I am very sick; but in the instant that   150
your messenger came, in loving visitation was with
me a young doctor of Rome; his name is Balthazar. I
acquainted him with the cause[65] in controversy between
the Jew and Antonio the merchant. We turned o'er
many books together. He is furnished with my
opinion; which, bettered with his own learning — the
greatness whereof I cannot enough commend — comes

[65]case

Ballerio is too sick to come.

A man is coming to give a judgement.

⁶⁶urging
⁶⁷instead of me

⁶⁸reputation

with him, at my importunity,⁶⁶ to fill up your Grace's
request in my stead.⁶⁷ I beseech you, let his lack of
years be no impediment to let him lack a reverend
estimation,⁶⁸ for I never knew so young a body with so
old a head. I leave him to your gracious acceptance, whose trial
shall better publish his
commendation.

                    Enter Portia, dressed like a doctor of law

You hear the learn'd Bellario, what he writes:
And here, I take it, is the doctor come.
Give me your hand. Come you from old Bellario?

Portia

I did, my lord.

Duke

          You are welcome: take your place.
⁶⁹dispute

Are you acquainted with the difference⁶⁹
That holds this present question in the court?

Portia

⁷⁰thoroughly

I am informed throughly⁷⁰ of the cause.
Which is the merchant here, and which the Jew?

Duke

Antonio and old Shylock, both stand forth.

Portia

Is your name Shylock?

Shylock

                    Shylock is my name.

Portia

Of a strange nature is the suit you follow;
Yet in such rule, that the Venetian law
⁷¹fault

⁷²in his power

Cannot impugn⁷¹ you as you do proceed.
[To Antonio] You stand within his danger,⁷² do you not?   180

Antonio

Ay, so he says.

Portia

                    Do you confess the bond?

Antonio

I do.

Portia

                    Then must the Jew be merciful.

Shylock

On what compulsion must I? tell me that.

[handwritten margin notes: "Do you know what the case is? about?" "170" "Yes" "Your weird."]

Portia

The quality of mercy is not strain'd;[73]
It droppeth as the gentle rain from heaven
Upon the place beneath: it is twice bless'd;
It blesseth him that gives and him that takes.
'Tis mightiest in the mightiest: it becomes[74]
The throned monarch better than his crown;
His sceptre shows the force of temporal[75] power,   190
The attribute to[76] awe and majesty,
Wherein doth sit the dread and fear of kings:
But mercy is above this sceptred sway,[77]
It is enthroned in the hearts of kings,
It is an attribute to God himself,
And earthly power doth then show likest God's
When mercy seasons[78] justice. Therefore, Jew,
Though justice be thy plea, consider this,
That in the course of justice none of us
Should see salvation: we do pray for mercy,
And that same prayer doth teach us all to render   200
The deeds of mercy. I have spoke thus much
To mitigate[79] the justice of thy plea,
Which if thou follow, this strict court of Venice
Must needs[80] give sentence 'gainst the merchant
    there.

Shylock

My deeds upon my head! I crave the law,
The penalty and forfeit of my bond.

Portia

Is he not able to discharge[81] the money?

Bassanio

Yes, here I tender[82] it for him in the court;
Yea, twice the sum: if that will not suffice,   210
I will be bound to pay it ten times o'er,
On forfeit of my hands, my head, my heart.
If this will not suffice, it must appear
That malice bears down[83] truth. And, I beseech you,
Wrest[84] once the law to your authority:
To do a great right, do a little wrong,
And curb this cruel devil of his will.

Portia

It must not be. There is no power in Venice
Can alter a decree established:
'Twill be recorded for a precedent,   220

[73] cannot be forced

[74] suits

[75] earthly
[76] the characteristic of

[77] the realm that is ruled by men with sceptres

[78] tempers, moderates

[79] to soften, reduce

[80] will have to

[81] pay

[82] offer

[83] overcomes
[84] bend

Handwritten annotations:
- Mercy cannot be forced
- Mercy is best from someone powerful
- No!
- I'll pay please find a loophole
- I can't

And many an error by the same example
Will rush into the state. It cannot be.

Shylock

[85] a young judge from the Old Testament whose name means 'God is my judge'. Daniel saved Susanna when she was falsely accused and gave judgment against the elders

A Daniel[85] come to judgment! yea, a Daniel!
O wise young judge, how I do honour thee!

Portia

I pray you, let me look upon the bond.

Shylock

Here 'tis, most reverend doctor, here it is.

Portia

Shylock, there's thrice thy money offer'd thee.

Shylock

[86] a lie told under oath

An oath, an oath, I have an oath in heaven;
Shall I lay perjury[86] upon my soul?
No, not for Venice.

I took a promise to heaven

Portia

      Why, this bond is forfeit;
And lawfully by this the Jew may claim
A pound of flesh, to be by him cut off
Nearest the merchant's heart. Be merciful:
Take thrice thy money; bid me tear the bond.

You can have it but 230 please take the money.

Shylock

[87] conditions laid down

When it is paid according to the tenour.[87]
It doth appear you are a worthy judge;
You know the law, your exposition
Hath been most sound: I charge you by the law,
Whereof you are a well-deserving pillar,
Proceed to judgment: by my soul I swear
There is no power in the tongue of man
To alter me. I stay here on my bond.

No!

240

Antonio

Most heartily I do beseech the court
To give the judgment.

Hurry up

Portia

      Why then, thus it is:
You must prepare your bosom for his knife.

Get ready

Shylock

O noble judge! O excellent young man!

Portia

[88] fully applies

For, the intent and purpose of the law
Hath full relation[88] to the penalty,
Which here appeareth due upon the bond.

Shylock

'Tis very true! O wise and upright judge!   *250*
How much more elder art thou than thy looks!

Portia

Therefore lay bare your bosom.

Shylock

      Ay, 'his breast':
So says the bond: — doth it not, noble judge? —
'Nearest his heart' — those are the very words.

Portia

It is so. Are there balance[89] here to weigh   [89]scales
The flesh?

Shylock

      I have them ready.

Portia

Have by some surgeon, Shylock, on your charge,[90]   [90]at your own expense
To stop his wounds, lest he do bleed to death.

Shylock

Is it so nominated[91] in the bond?   [91]specified

Portia

It is not so express'd; but what of that?   *260*
'Twere good you do so much for charity.

Shylock

I cannot find it: 'tis not in the bond.

Portia

You, merchant, have you anything to say?

Antonio

But little: I am arm'd and well prepar'd.
Give me your hand, Bassanio: fare you well!
Grieve not that I am fall'n to this for you,
For herein Fortune shows herself more kind
Than is her custom: it is still her use[92]   [92]custom
To let the wretched man outlive his wealth,
To view with hollow eye and wrinkled brow   *270*
An age of poverty; from which lingering penance
Of such misery doth she cut me off.
Commend me to your honourable wife.
Tell her the process of Antonio's end;
Say how I lov'd you, speak me fair in death;[93]   [93]speak kindly of me when I
And, when the tale is told, bid her be judge   am dead

Whether Bassanio had not once a love.

[94]regret only

Repent but you[94] that you shall lose your friend,
And he repents not that he pays your debt;
For if the Jew do cut but deep enough,
I'll pay it instantly with all my heart.   280

Don't worry

I'd give anything to save you.

Bassanio

Antonio, I am married to a wife

[95]who

Which[95] is as dear to me as life itself;
But life itself, my wife, and all the world,
Are not with me esteem'd above thy life:
I would lose all, ay, sacrifice them all,
Here to this devil, to deliver you.

Portia

Your wife would give you little thanks for that,
If she were by to hear you make the offer.

Gratiano

I have a wife, who, I protest, I love: 290
I would she were in heaven, so she could
Entreat some power to change this currish Jew.

If she heard, there'd be a row.

Nerissa

'Tis well you offer it behind her back;
The wish would make else an unquiet house.

Shylock

These be the Christian husbands! I have a
    daughter;

[96]Jewish race

Would any of the stock of Barabas[96]
Had been her husband rather than a Christian!

[97]waste

We trifle[97] time; I pray thee, pursue sentence.

Portia

A pound of that same merchant's flesh is thine:
The court awards it, and the law doth give it.   300

Shylock

Most rightful judge!

Portia

And you must cut this flesh from off his breast:
The law allows it, and the court awards it.

Shylock

Most learned judge! A sentence! come, prepare!

Portia

[98]wait a moment

Tarry a little:[98] there is something else.
This bond doth give thee here no jot of blood;
The words expressly are 'a pound of flesh':

Take then thy bond, take thou thy pound of flesh;
But, in the cutting it, if thou dost shed
One drop of Christian blood, thy lands and goods
Are, by the laws of Venice, confiscate
Unto the state of Venice.

If you take any, you're blood in trouble

310

Gratiano

O upright judge! Mark, Jew: O learned judge!

Throwing the words back at Shylock

Shylock

Is that the law?

Portia

    Thyself shalt see the act;
For, as thou urgest justice, be assur'd
Thou shalt have justice more than thou desir'st.

It will be done as you want

Gratiano

O learned judge! Mark, Jew: a learned judge!

Shylock

I take this offer then: pay the bond thrice,
And let the Christian go.

Bassanio

    Here is the money.

320

Portia

Soft!
The Jew shall have all justice; soft! no haste:
He shall have nothing but the penalty.

No this is what Shylock wanted.

Gratiano

O Jew! an upright judge, a learned judge!

Portia

Therefore prepare thee to cut off the flesh.
Shed thou no blood; nor cut thou less, nor more,
But just a pound of flesh: if thou tak'st more,
Or less, than a just[99] pound, be it but so much
As makes it light or heavy in the substance,[100]
Or the division of the twentieth part
Of one poor scruple,[101] nay, if the scale do turn
But in the estimation[102] of a hair,
Thou diest, and all thy goods are confiscate.

One piece = wrong amount Shylock dies and his goods taken

[99]exact
[100]amount

330

[101]a very small unit of
  weight
[102]measurement

Gratiano

A second Daniel, a Daniel, Jew!
Now, infidel, I have you on the hip.[103]

Portia

Why doth the Jew pause? take thy forfeiture.

Go ahead

[103]at a disadvantage, i.e. at
  my mercy

Shylock

Give me my principal, and let me go.   *Give me the original amount.*

Bassanio

I have it ready for thee; here it is.

Portia

He hath refus'd it in the open court: *No. Just his*
He shall have merely justice, and his bond.   *bond.*   340

Gratiano

A Daniel, still say I; a second Daniel!
I thank thee, Jew, for teaching me that word.

Shylock

Shall I not have barely my principal?

Portia

Thou shalt have nothing but the forfeiture,   *Be careful.*
To be so taken at thy peril, Jew.   *risk*

Shylock

Why, then the devil give him good of it!   *I'm leaving.*
I'll stay no longer question.[104]

Portia   *wait*

    Tarry, Jew:
The law hath yet another hold on you.
It is enacted in the laws of Venice,
If it be prov'd against an alien
That by direct or indirect attempts   *He loses half*
He seek the life of any citizen,   *to Antonio*   350
The party[105] 'gainst the which he doth contrive[106] *and*
Shall seize one half his goods; the other half *half to*
Comes to the privy coffer[107] of the state;   *the state.*
And the offender's life lies in the mercy   *Duke decides*
Of the duke only, 'gainst all other voice.[108] *if Shylock*
In which predicament,[109] I say, thou stand'st; *lives or*
For it appears by manifest proceeding,[110]   *dies.*   360
That indirectly, and directly too,
Thou hast contriv'd against the very life
Of the defendant; and thou hast incurr'd
The danger formerly by me rehears'd,[111]
Down therefore and beg mercy of the duke.

Gratiano

Beg that thou may'st have leave to hang thyself —   *He will be*
And yet, thy wealth being forfeit to the state,   *in death to*
Thou hast not left the value of a cord;   *the state*
Therefore thou must be hang'd at the state's charge. *even if*

he commits suicide

[104]to argue

[105]person
[106]plot

[107]private treasury

[108]in spite of what anyone
    else says
[109]situation
[110]from what has clearly
    happened

[111]explained

Duke

That thou shalt see the difference of our spirit,
I pardon thee thy life before thou ask it.   *half to state half to Antonio* 370
For half thy wealth, it is Antonio's;
The other half comes to the general state,
Which humbleness may drive[112] unto a fine.   [112]commute, reduce

Portia

Ay, for the state; not for Antonio.

Shylock

Nay, take my life and all; pardon not that:
You take my house, when you do take the prop   *Just kill me*
That doth sustain my house; you take my life
When you do take the means whereby I live.

Portia

What mercy can you render him, Antonio?

Gratiano

A halter gratis;[113] nothing else, for God's sake!   *A rope*   380   [113]rope free of charge, i.e.
                                                                                                  to hang himself with

Antonio

So please my lord the duke, and all the court,
To quit[114] the fine for one half of his goods,   *Just give half to Jessica and Lorenzo and all when he dies*   [114]to remit
I am content so he will let me have
The other half in use,[115] to render it,   [115]in trust
Upon his death, unto the gentleman
That lately stole his daughter.
Two things provided more, that, for this favour,
He presently[116] become a Christian;   [116]immediately
The other, that he do record a gift,   *Change religion*
Here in the court, of all he dies possess'd,[117]   390   [117]that he possesses when
Unto his son Lorenzo and his daughter.   he dies

Duke

He shall do this, or else I do recant[118]   *If not he dies.*   [118]retract, withdraw
The pardon that I late pronounced here.

Portia

Art thou contented, Jew? what dost thou say?   *Ok?*

Shylock

I am content.   *Yes*

Portia

              Clerk, draw a deed of gift.   *make a contract*

Shylock

I pray you give me leave to go from hence: *Can't go further. send it to me and ill sigh it*
I am not well. Send the deed after me,
And I will sign it.

Duke

Get thee gone, but do it.

Gratiano

In christening shalt thou have two god-fathers;
Had I been judge, thou shouldst have had ten more[119]   400
To bring thee to the gallows, not to the font.

[Exit Shylock

Duke

Sir, I entreat you home with me to dinner.

Portia

I humbly do desire your Grace of pardon:
I must away this night toward Padua,
And it is meet[120] presently set forth.

Sorry I can't

Duke

I am sorry that your leisure serves you not.[121]
Antonio, gratify[122] this gentleman,
For, in my mind, you are much bound[123] to him.

Pay Portia.

[Exeunt Duke, Merchants and Officers of the Court

Bassanio

Most worthy gentleman, I and my friend
Have by your wisdom been this day acquitted
Of grievous penalties, in lieu whereof,[124]
Three thousand ducats, due unto the Jew,
We freely cope your courteous pains withal.[125]

Three thousand ducats 410

Antonio

And stand indebted, over and above,
In love and service to you evermore.

Portia

He is well paid that is well satisfied,
And I, delivering you, am satisfied,
And therein do account myself well paid:
My mind was never yet more mercenary.[126]
I pray you, know me when we meet again:
I wish you well, and so I take my leave.

I'm happy I did the right thing 420

Bassanio

Dear sir, of force[127] must attempt[128] you further:
Take some remembrance[129] of us as a tribute,[130]
Not as a fee. Grant me two things, I pray you,
Not to deny me, and to pardon me.

Take a gift then

Portia

You press me far, and therefore I will yield.

[119]jury of twelve

[120]necessary that

[121]you have not more time at your disposal
[122]show your gratitude to
[123]greatly indebted

[124]in return for which

[125]we willingly reward your kind efforts with

[126]money-minded

[127]of necessity
[128]attempt to persuade
[129]memento
[130]an acknowledgement

Give me your gloves, I'll wear them for your sake;
And (for your love) I'll take this ring from you.
Do not draw back your hand; I'll take no more,
And you in love shall not deny me this.

Give me the ring

Bassanio

This ring, good sir? alas! it is a trifle,
I will not shame myself to give you this.

You don't want this

430

Portia

I will have nothing else but only this;
And now methinks I have a mind to it.[131]

I want it more now.

[131]my mind is really set on it

Bassanio

There's more depends on this than on the value.
The dearest ring in Venice will I give you,
And find it out by proclamation;[132]
Only for this, I pray you, pardon me.

I'll get you a better one.

[132]by public announcement

Portia

I see, sir, you are liberal in offers:
You taught me first to beg, and now methinks[133]
You teach me how a beggar should be answer'd.

440

[133]it seems to me that

Bassanio

Good sir, this ring was given me by my wife,
And, when she put it on, she made me vow
That I should neither sell, nor give, nor lose it.

Portia

That 'scuse[134] serves many men to save their gifts.
And if your wife be not a mad-woman,
And know how well I have deserv'd this ring,
She would not hold out enemy[135] for ever,
For giving it to me. Well, peace be with you.

That's an excuse!

[134]excuse

[135]remain hostile

[Exeunt Portia and Nerissa

Antonio

My Lord Bassanio, let him have the ring:
Let his deservings and my love withal[136]
Be valu'd 'gainst your wife's commandèment.

Can't say no to Antonio

450

[136]as well

Bassanio

Go, Gratiano; run and overtake him;
Give him the ring, and bring him, if thou canst,
Unto Antonio's house. Away, make haste.

Go after him

[Exit Gratiano

Gratiano

Come, you and I will thither[137] presently,
And in the morning early will we both
Fly toward Belmont. Come, Antonio.

[137]go there

[Exeunt

Summary

The Trial

In a Venetian court of justice Shylock's case against Antonio is about to be heard. Antonio is summoned first and the Duke, who is presiding over the court, offers him sympathy on account of the inhumanity and heartlessness of the adversary he faces.

Antonio acknowledges the efforts the Duke has made to moderate Shylock's demands but since Shylock remains hard-hearted, Antonio is prepared for what is coming.

Shylock is now called before the court and the Duke asks him to show mercy to Antonio. Shylock has carried the pretence of cruelty far enough in the Duke's opinion and Antonio has already suffered enough.

Shylock refuses to show mercy: he has been serious in his demands and he will discredit the Venetian legal system if he does not have his pound of flesh. He gives no reason for his insistence other than that it is his humour: he wants it and that is that. Just as some people hate roast pig's head, or cats or the drones of the bagpipes, so he hates Antonio and as he explains in the exchange with Bassanio that follows, he believes that if someone hates something he will be prepared to kill it.

Antonio tells Bassanio that he might as well be trying to stop the tide as to be arguing with Shylock; enough has been said and the sooner the judgment is given the better. Bassanio offers Shylock twice the sum involved in the bond but Shylock will not settle at any price for anything less than the pound of flesh.

The Duke asks Shylock what mercy he can expect if he shows none. Shylock replies that he has done nothing wrong and if Christians can abuse their slaves simply because they own them, he can also do whatever he likes with a pound of flesh that legally belongs to him.

At this point the Duke says that he will adjourn proceedings unless a famous lawyer called Bellario arrives to give his opinion. As it happens, Bellario's messenger is outside and while they wait for him Bassanio tries to rouse Antonio's downcast spirits. He even offers to die in his friend's place. Antonio asks Bassanio to drop the issue: he himself is like a diseased ram and is more suited to dying than Bassanio who should look after himself and live to write Antonio's epitaph.

Nerissa enters the court dressed as a lawyer's clerk with a letter from Bellario to the Duke. As the Duke reads the letter, Shylock sharpens his knife on the sole of his shoe to the horror of Gratiano who accuses Shylock of being a wolf masquerading as a human being. Shylock tells Gratiano that he is wasting his breath because the law is on Shylock's side.

Bellario has written that he is too ill to attend the court and that he is sending in his place a young lawyer called Balthazar who is well briefed on the case and whose opinion should not be valued any less because of his youthful appearance.

Balthazar is none other than Portia, but as she enters the court no one other than Nerissa is aware of her true identity. Portia addresses the court and the adversaries. She is familiar with the details of the case and can find no fault in the proceedings: as far as she is concerned Shylock is within his legal rights to press the case and all she can ask of him is that he be merciful. Shylock wants to know why he should be merciful and this prompts Portia into an eloquent speech on the subject of mercy. Mercy, she says, is a gentle quality which enobles the man who shows it as much as the man who receives it. It is something that comes from the heart and is superior to mere justice or kingly power. Mercy is above all an attribute of God, without whose infinite mercy sinful mankind would be damned. Portia commends mercy to Shylock because it is fitting that men should display towards each other the same mercy which they receive from God.

Shylock is unimpressed by Portia's Christian eloquence: he would rather have the letter of Venetian law. Bassanio offers more and more of Portia's money to Shylock and begs Portia to bend the law a little. Portia replies that she cannot tamper with an established law. Shylock praises Portia's wisdom and compares her to Daniel, an Old Testament youth who gave judgment against his elders.

Portia finally examines the bond itself and asks Shylock if he will not take Bassanio's offer of three times the sum of money mentioned in the bond. Shylock insists on the pound of flesh once more and Portia rules that he is entitled to it. Shylock wants a formal judgment without further delay and when Antonio supports this request Portia instructs him to prepare his chest for Shylock's knife. Shylock demands that the terms of the penalty be carried out to the last letter and that the flesh be taken from the area around Antonio's heart. Portia calls for a scales to weigh the flesh and Shylock has one ready. He does not see, however, why he should bow to Portia's suggestion that he have a surgeon ready in case Antonio bleeds to death; it is not in the bond and therefore is an irrelevance.

Antonio is given the opportunity of saying a last few words. He turns to Bassanio and bids him an emotional farewell. He does not want Bassanio to regret anything other than losing a friend. He asks that he be remembered to Bassanio's wife.

Portia and Nerissa raise their eyebrows as Bassanio and Gratiano in quick succession say that they would sacrifice everything – even their wives – to save Antonio! Portia and Nerissa doubt whether the two wives in question would relish such an offer! Shylock, of course, does not think very highly of Christian husbands anyway.

The dreaded moment has arrived and Shylock prepares to cut Antonio's flesh. But before he can begin, there is a sensational development. Portia cautions him that while he may have his pound of flesh, no provision has been made in the bond for a single drop of Antonio's blood. If Shylock takes anything over and above what is nominated in the words of the bond he stands to have all his property confiscated.

As the tables are turned on Shylock, Gratiano gloats triumphantly, repeating with sneering irony the words of praise which Shylock heaped on Portia when things were going his way.

Shylock is quick to sum up that he has been foiled and decides to settle for the money that has been offered and which Bassanio is prepared to give. But Portia decides that the law must have its course and that Shylock may have nothing other than the flesh nominated in the bond – and that only at his peril. Since he has refused money, money is no longer on offer – not even the original amount borrowed.

Shylock knows he is utterly defeated and wants to leave. His humiliation, however, is only beginning. As an alien in Venice who has sought the life of a citizen, his possessions are to be confiscated and his life placed at the discretion of the Duke. The Duke spares Shylock's life and offers some leniency if humility is displayed. But Shylock at this stage would rather die.

Portia asks Antonio to decide what mercy is to be shown to Shylock. Antonio, for his own part, will be satisfied with half of Shylock's estate which he will keep in trust for Jessica. Shylock may retain the other half of his estate provided that he becomes a Christian and signs a deed leaving everything he owns to Jessica and Lorenzo at his death.

Shylock is a broken man. He agrees meekly to the conditions imposed on him and asks the court's permission to leave because he is ill. Gratiano continues to jeer him as he leaves.

The Duke asks Portia to his home for dinner but being pressed for time she declines. He tells Bassanio to show his gratitude to Portia, and Bassanio offers her the 3,000 ducats which were due to Shylock. Portia refuses courteously to take what is after all her own money. She has no interest in money and merely wishes to be remembered when next they meet! Bassanio insists that she take some token of their gratitude. She asks for his gloves and when he has removed them she asks for the ring on his finger. He tries to explain to her that it is the one thing he cannot part with. Portia presses for the ring, however, and tells Bassanio that his wife could not be angry with him for very long in the circumstances. When the ring is not forthcoming she turns and leaves as if offended. Antonio shames Bassanio into sending Gratiano after the lawyer with the ring.

Antonio and Bassanio will return to Belmont in the morning, having spent the night at Antonio's house.

Scene Analysis

A Very Famous Scene

The trial scene in *The Merchant of Venice* is one of the most famous scenes in all dramatic literature. It has given the phrase *'a pound of flesh'* to the English language. It is the dramatic high point of the play which brings all the major characters together for the first time. Shylock's lust for revenge encounters Portia's nimble intellect in a critical duel which determines the outcome of the play.

The quality of mercy is not strain'd,
It droppeth as the gentle rain from heaven
Upon the place beneath.   *(Portia, Act 4, Sc I)*

Tension

The scene is filled with tension. Our anxiety at the apparent hopelessness of Antonio's case and at the determination of Shylock to murder him legally is fanned by Portia's legal coldness and seeming agreement with Shylock. She keeps poor Antonio on tenterhooks for a very long time. The tension reaches its high point as Shylock sharpens his knife on the sole of his shoe and Portia asks Antonio to open his doublet and prepare for an incision.

Comedy

Despite the tension, however, there is much humour in the scene although almost all of it is tinged with irony. Shylock eagerly produces for Portia the bond that will be his undoing and applauds the wisdom of the judge who is about to ruin him: he examines the bond with grotesque interest to verify that flesh must be taken from nearest Antonio's heart and searches in vain for any mention of a surgeon: he speedily asks for the money when his claim to flesh is disallowed. The humour in these images of Shylock suggests that, in the midst of tension, the scene really has a comic purpose and a comic outcome.

The most constant source of humour is the comic confusion of identity arising out of Portia and Nerissa's disguise. No one recognises Portia – not even her husband who cannot calculate the effect a nobly impulsive gesture will have on the young lawyer before him:

> '*But life itself, my wife, and all the world,*
> *Are not with me esteem'd above thy life:*
> *I would lose all, ay, sacrifice them all,*
> *Here to this devil, to deliver you.*'

Portia's reply is as wry as it is abrupt:

> '*Your wife would give you little thanks for that,*
> *If she were by to hear you make the offer.*'

> *A Daniel come to judgment! yea, a Daniel!*
> *O wise young judge, how I do honour thee!*   (Shylock, Act 4, Sc I)

Gratiano's repetition of Bassanio's gesture and Nerissa's icy response duplicate and underline the humour and Shylock, of all people, rounds off the comic exchange:

> '*These be the Christian husbands!*'

At the very high point of crisis Shakespeare is reminding us that his play is a comedy and not a tragedy.

A Comic Reversal Of Fortunes

There is something comic also in the denouement of the scene which is about to occur. The crux comes in the line where Portia says to Shylock:

> *'Tarry a little: there is something else.'*

What is about to happen has that irony and humour which is attached to poetic justice: the villain is about to get a large dose of his own medicine. In speech after speech, Shakespeare has prepared us for the moment when Shylock's insistence on the letter of the law will be turned against him. When Portia says, *'The Jew shall have all justice;'* it is his own version of justice that she has in mind for him.

> *'This bond doth give thee here no jot of blood;*
> *The words expressly are "a pound of flesh":'*

Shylock gets the letter of the law with a vengeance:

> *'if thou tak'st more,*
> *Or less, than a just pound, let it be so much*
> *As makes it light or heavy in the substance,*
> *Or the division of the twentieth part*
> *Of one poor scruple, nay, if the scale do turn*
> *But in the estimation of a hair,*
> *Thou diest, and all thy goods are confiscate.'*

These lines, spoken by Portia, are a grim parody of Shylock. The insane obsession with precision which they reveal shows us what mere *'justice'* looks like when it is taken to its logical conclusion: it is totally devoid of humanity or common sense.

Theme: A Plea For Tolerance

The theme of the scene is the inhumanity of mere justice. The mere letter of the law can be barbaric if it is not tempered with the spirit of the law which encompasses mercy and ordinary humanity.

Fair Play!

But has justice really been served? If there was something outrageous in Shylock's demands, is there not something equally outrageous in his defeat? Has not every known principle of jurisprudence been made nonsense of and is there not an extent to which the whole scene is an ingenious satire on justice and courts of law?

Legally and logically it would appear that Shylock was entitled to shed blood in getting payment of the penalty owed. Surely the right to perform a certain act (cutting a pound of flesh) confers the right to the necessary incidents of that act (shedding blood). And surely anyone who has the right to take a certain amount of anything has the right also to take less.

There is also the question of whether the punishment meted out to Shylock was appropriate to the crime. It certainly seems somewhat disproportionate. No doubt the Elizabethan Christian audience would have seen Shylock's enforced conversion as being for the good of his soul and therefore merciful. But today we regard the right to one's faith as sacrosanct and whatever about the confiscation of property, we would look askance at the way Shylock is forced to abandon his Jewish faith and become a Christian.

There is therefore an extent to which the contrived illegality of Shylock's defeat and the callous quality in the way he is treated indicts Christian hypocrisy and makes it difficult for us to share totally in the exultation of his victors. Shylock gets little of the mercy which we heard so much about and there is an unseeming haste in the manner in which his Christian victors get on with their lives as if nothing had happened.

The pound of flesh which I demand of him,
is dearly bought; 'tis mine and I will have it.   (Shylock, Act 4, Sc I)

Life Goes On

Whatever the justice of it, the Jew has been destroyed, Antonio has been saved and the lovers are free to return to their blissful world of love and concord. There is an extent to which the play is over: after the denouement, little of dramatic importance remains and in the stage history of the play a number of famous productions ended with Shylock's exit.

Yet Shakespeare chose not to end the play here and we must respect his wishes. In the ring plot which now unfolds and through the final act, comedy and romance are given a chance to triumph emphatically over the darker world which Shylock personified.

If thou dost shed
One drop of Christian blood, thy lands and goods
Are, by the laws of Venice, confiscate
Unto the state of Venice.   *(Portia, Act 4, Sc I)*

Characters

A LAST LOOK AT SHYLOCK

Shylock has come to court with a knife and a scales and the **butcher** in him gives very little scope for sympathy: it is difficult to sentimentalise a man who has a taste for legal murder:

> *'...I rather choose to have*
> *A weight of carrion flesh than to receive*
> *Three thousand ducats.'*

Shylock nevertheless enters the court with a certain amount of **dignity**. He is not overawed by a Duke who sympathises with his adversary nor is he intimidated by the enemies who surround him on all sides. He is quite unimpressed, in fact, by the might and grandeur of the Venetian legal world assembled before him:

> *'If you deny me, fie upon your law!*
> *There is no force in the decrees of Venice.'*

What we notice most about Shylock in the trial scene is **the unmoved and unrelenting manner in which he demands his bond**. He turns down every opportunity to relent and remains an *'unfeeling man'* who *'stands obdurate'*, a *'stony adversary'* comparable to the cold rocks which have wrecked Antonio's ships. He says of himself:

> *'There is no power in the tongue of man*
> *To alter me.'*

Antonio sees only too well the futility of trying to alter Shylock:

> *'You may as well use question with the wolf,*
> *Why he hath made the ewe bleat for the lamb;'*

Antonio has lapsed into animal imagery in describing Shylock's inhuman obduracy and Gratiano goes even further: he sees Shylock as a man who has lapsed into an animal –*'an inexorable dog'* with a *'currish spirit'* whose:

> *'...desires*
> *Are wolvish, bloody, starv'd and ravenous.'*

Shylock makes little effort to explain to anyone his *'wolvish'* appetite for *'carrion flesh'*. His implacable *'humour'* is all he offers:

> *'...I give no reason, nor I will not,*
> *More than a lodg'd hate and a certain loathing*
> *I bear Antonio,'*

His **motive is quite simply revenge** and the instrument whereby he will achieve his revenge is **the law**. Law will vindicate him for all the agonies he has suffered.

'I crave the law', is his recurring theme. He is legally and logically on solid ground and he knows it. In a voice which is almost noble in its righteousness, he demands adherance to the law which was made by those who now want to evade it. Shylock fears nothing because law is on his side.

> *'I stand here for law.'*

He is so confident that his position is unassailable that he positively invites retribution:

> *'My deeds upon my head!'* he says, and, *'What judgment shall I dread, doing no wrong?'*

Shylock's view of the law makes it a very appropriate instrument for revenge – an eye for an eye. Justice involves ruthless and automatic implementing of the letter of the law: the spirit of the law is not part of Shylock's philosophy. His literal and mechanical way of seeing things leaves little room for the common sense which the Duke urges or the mercy which Portia advocates.

> 'Is it so nominated in the bond?'

he asks, when Portia asks him to provide a surgeon to save Antonio's life. Whatever is not written down in black and white is irrelevant to Shylock:

> '"Nearest his heart" — those are the very words.'

As we have seen, a comic **reversal** befalls the villain who is defeated by the very legalism he insisted on. In whatever metaphor you prefer to choose, Shylock turns the tables on Shylock, digs his own grave, nooses himself, gives his enemies the grounds on which he is defeated. He even gives them the words with which he is whipped:

> 'A Daniel come to judgment!'

> 'I thank thee, Jew,' Gratiano says, 'for teaching me that word.'

Shylock's defeat is as total as it is sudden and he sees the writing on the wall very quickly:

> "Why, then the devil give him good of it!
> I'll stay no longer question.'

We remember the words of the Duke as Shylock is humiliated:

> 'How shalt thou hope for mercy, rendering none?'

Shylock receives little mercy and Gratiano's cruel taunting rubs salt into his wounds:

> 'Beg that thou may'st have leave to hang thyself.'

Shylock's enemies have walked all over him and he leaves the court a sad and ruined man.

> 'I pray you give me leave to go from hence:
> I am not well.'

The words have a quiet dignity and an understated pathos whose eloquence is underlined by the contrasting shallowness of the petty concerns to which his victors so hastily return. The alien has been defeated and life returns to normal, but in defeat Shylock haunts the imagination and casts a shadow across the comedy and romance of which the remainder of the play is made.

Postscript: An Epitaph For Shylock

The way we see Shylock determines how we see the whole play. The fundamental question may be whether Shylock was more sinned against than sinning, and whether we give a tough or tender interpretation to his character depends on our answer to that question. Some see in Shylock a pure villain while others see him as a tragic figure, a potentially noble nature twisted and thwarted by a society that has no moral core.

The play makes little sense if Shylock is not a villain and Shakespeare with little doubt set out to portray him as such. But there is no doubt also that Shylock transcends the villain moneylender of popular legend which Shakespeare set out to portray. He goes beyond the boundaries of cliché and convention and is so endowed with organs, dimensions, senses, affections and passions that he engages our imaginative understanding and sometimes our sympathy. Yet he remains a villain: while we sympathise with him for the agonies behind his hatred and see in him the ghettoised representative of a persecuted race, we nevertheless recognise how twisted he is in his values and that what he seeks in the end puts him almost outside the pale of what is human. Certainly in another time and place, perhaps upon a different stage, he might have been a tragic figure, and certainly there is something tragic about him: but we must not let these things cloud over the fact that he is the villain of the play.

Whatever we think of him, he is the central figure in *The Merchant of Venice*. He is the strongest and most vibrant character in the play and he gives it a texture and flavour without which it might all be so much fantasy – even nonsense. He is one of the greatest characters to come out of the human imagination onto the pages of fiction and he is so three dimensional that we can imagine him outside and beyond the five short scenes to which his author confined him. He is a supreme challenge to the actor and a list of those who gave a new twist or slant to his character reads like a history of the greatest actors to have graced the stage – Richard Burbage and Charles Macklin in the 18th century, Edmund Kean and Henry Irving in the 19th, John Gielgud, Peter O'Toole, Laurence Olivier and Cyril Cusack in the 20th and Al Pacino in our own century. He is a challenge which remains.

PORTIA IN THE TRIAL SCENE

Portia has hatched the audacious plan that she be the **arbitrator** in the case of Shylock against Antonio and she carries it off with consummate **assurance** and **matter-of-factness.** She is *'informed throughly of the cause'* and upholds Venetian law with such **authority** that she wins Shylock's approval.

> *'O wise and upright judge!*
> *How much more elder art thou than thy looks!'*

Though there can be no doubt where Portia's sympathy lies, she endeavours to remain that **principled** lady who adhered to her father's will through thick and thin: when her legal coldness drives an exasperated Bassanio to suggest that she *'do a little wrong"* to save Antonio, she replies:

> *'...There is no power in Venice*
> *Can alter a decree established:'*

Portia is so **totally in command** of the situation that she is able to indulge in some of that subtle wit which we saw when she dissected her unwanted suitors in Act 1, Scene II. The object of her **ironic humour** now, however, is the man she loves and his noble sentiments about sacrificing a woman he believes to be far away:

> *'Your wife would give you little thanks for that,*
> *If she were by to hear you to make the offer.'*

It is a **mock disgust** that we will find her returning to later in the ring plot which ends the scene: she knows Bassanio's heart is in the right place and she secretly approves of his noble gesture, but she cannot resist enjoying the comedy of her disguise and playing games with her lover while she has him in her power – even in the midst of a critical intellectual struggle.

Portia's most famous lines in the whole play are in her eloquent speech on *'mercy'*:

> *'The quality of mercy is not strain'd;*
> *It droppeth as the gentle rain from heaven*
> *Upon the place beneath:'*

If the poetry of these lines did not win Shylock's heart, it has certainly won the hearts of anthologists ever since. Her words are redolent of the Lord's Prayer and add up to the most Christian statement in all of Shakespeare. Her **theme** is that *'mercy seasons justice'* and that giving *'blesseth him that gives'.*

It is one of the major themes of the play and suggests that Antonio's generosity will win out in the end.

Shakespeare's first lady of the Renaissance renders a worthy account of herself as far as wit, intelligence and eloquence are concerned. **But not everyone finds in her the almost divine heroine she is sometimes made out to be.**

Portia's detractors point especially to the **venom** with which she turns the tables on Shylock. She out-Shylocks Shylock with a deadly thoroughness that is chilling and releases upon him the full terrors of the law he has evoked.

> *'Thou shalt have justice more than thou desir'st.'*

Every move she makes is totally deliberate:

> 'The Jew shall have all justice; soft! no haste:'

There is a new **tone** in her voice which is **coldly vindictive** and her words exhibit a remorseless logic which is as inflexible as Shylock at his worst. Even when the Duke offers to reduce the state's claim upon Shylock's wealth, Portia is adamantly unyielding:

> 'Ay, for the state; not for Antonio.'

What is perhaps worst of all is that her words are laced with the language of prejudice :

> 'Art thou contented, Jew?' she sneers at Shylock.

The word 'Jew' is reiterated with unmistakable malevolence: he is the 'alien' who will not get 'One drop of Christian blood'.

There is no doubt whose side Portia is on now.

Portia does to Shylock with law what Gratiano does with words and the cruelty of it leaves her open to the charge of **hypocrisy**. The lady who so recently advocated mercy that was as 'gentle' as the 'rain from heaven' seems deaf now to her own eloquence; or is it that she regards mercy as a virtue reserved only for gentiles? One of the first sentences that Portia uttered rings in our minds with renewed relevance:

> 'It is a good divine that follows his own instructions:'

We may finally ask ourselves how Portia can be so **callous and hard-hearted** as to be able to indulge in the perverse merriment of the ring plot so soon after the painful destruction of a man – no matter how villainous he may have been.

A number of things can be said in Portia's favour, however. **She gives Shylock every chance to save his own soul.** She asks him repeatedly to show mercy or at least charity. In a series of exchanges she establishes that he will not take money instead of flesh, that he has no surgeon to staunch Antonio's wounds but that he has a scales at hand and is ready and eager to cut into Antonio. It is only after Shylock refuses every chance to relent that Portia lets him have 'all justice'.

It can also be argued that Portia's **high spirits are understandable** on what is the happiest day of her life! She has satisfied her father's will, married the man she pined for and saved the life of his best friend. Her happiness is the inevitable consequence of the extreme emotional relief she is feeling.

It could also be said that **Portia is simply returning to being Portia** – that indomitable young lady who took girlish delight in poking fun at unwanted suitors and impersonating young men. That, the argument goes, is the real Portia and the ruthless Portia of the trial scene was a temporary but necessary role which did not show the true face of the woman who has a genuine instinct for kindness and mercy.

Whatever we think of these arguments, the final judgement on Portia is one which, in the last analysis, we shall have to make for ourselves.

BASSANIO

It was Bassanio's borrowing which put Antonio into Shylock's grasp in the first place and now **he has borrowed again** in order to salvage the situation. If Antonio sponsored his trip to Belmont, it is Portia who sponsors his return to Venice.

Bassanio has **no head for money, however:** if it comes to him easily it will go easily too.

> *'For thy three thousand ducats here is six.'*

is but his opening offer to Shylock:

> *'...if that will not suffice*
> *I will be bound to pay it ten times o'er,'*

Bassanio is willing to pay Shylock to the very end:

> *'I have it ready for thee; here it is.'*

When Shylock is defeated and gone, the money is still burning in Bassanio's pocket; he offers it to the *'Most worthy gentleman'* who has saved the day:

> *'Three thousand ducats, due unto the Jew,*
> *We freely cope your courteous pains withal.'*

Bassanio is so willing to part with Portia's money, not because it is Portia's, but because of his **inherent generosity.**

> *'The Jew shall have my flesh, blood, bones and all,*
> *Ere thou shalt lose for me one drop of blood.'*

Bassanio lives up to the motto on the lead casket he chose in winning Portia.

> *'Who chooseth me must give and hazard all he hath.'*

He was willing to sacrifice everything to gain Portia and now he is willing to *'lose all'* – Portia included – in order to save Antonio. It is the kind of generosity which can get a man into all kinds of trouble:

> *'Your wife would give you little thanks for that,*
> *If she were by to hear you make the offer.'*

As the scene ends, Bassanio's generosity has put him into an impossible situation with regard to his most treasured personal possession and his wife will be waiting once again to give him *'little thanks'.*

ANTONIO

Antonio **has lost all hope** of surviving Shylock's *'tyranny and rage'*. He simply wants to get it all over with:

> *'But with all brief and plain conveniency,*
> *Let me have judgment, and the Jew his will.'*

His **willingness to die** is almost a death wish and reflects again that morbid strain of melancholy in his character which we noted previously.

> *'I am a tainted wether of the flock,*
> *Meetest for death:'*

As his inevitable death draws near, however, Antonio assumes an air of **dignified nobility**. He is *'arm'd and well prepar'd'* for the end and his last act of generosity will be to absolve Bassanio of all guilt:

> *'Grieve not that I am fall'n to this for you,'*

When the crisis has passed, Antonio **shows no vindictiveness**. He asks the Duke to remit part of Shylock's penalty and is happy that Lorenzo and Jessica be the beneficiaries of Shylock's will. Though he believes himself to be financially ruined, he renounces his own share in Shylock's forfeited wealth in favour of the young lovers. A modern audience might be horrified that he forced Shylock to become a Christian, but Antonio would have seen it as guaranteeing the salvation of his old enemy. Antonio's reluctance to go too hard on Shylock shows perhaps that suffering has made him a more tolerant person than he used to be.

GRATIANO

Gratiano is never as dignified as Antonio or Bassanio. He is not burdened by any gentlemanly reserve and can speak his mind with such directness that Bassanio had to caution him in an earlier scene for being *'too wild, too rude, and bold of voice'*.

When he sees Shylock sharpening his knife on the sole of his shoe he is no longer able

> *'To allay with some cold drops of modesty'* – his *'skipping spirit'*. *'Thy desires'*, he says
> –*'Are wolfish, bloody, starv'd and ravenous.'*

The words that will hurt Shylock most, however, are the words he himself used and Gratiano throws them back at him with cruel sarcasm:

> *'O upright judge! Mark, Jew: O learned judge!'*

Gratiano is unashamedly vindicitive and he offers Shylock no mercy other than

> 'A halter gratis; nothing else, for God's sake!'

It is not difficult to see what Bassanio was referring to.

Scene II

Venice. A street
Enter Portia and Nerissa

Portia

Inquire the Jew's house out,[1] give him this deed,[2]
And let him sign it. We'll away tonight,
And be a day before our husbands home:
This deed will be well welcome to Lorenzo.

Enter Gratiano

Gratiano

Fair sir, you are well o'erta'en[3]
My Lord Bassanio, upon more advice,[4]
Hath sent you here this ring, and doth entreat[5]
Your company at dinner.

Portia

That cannot be.
His ring I do accept most thankfully,
And so, I pray you, tell him: furthermore,   10
I pray you, show my youth old Shylock's house.

Gratiano

That will I do.

Nerissa

.   Sir, I would speak with you.
[Aside to Portia] I'll see if I can get my husband's ring.
Which I did make him swear to keep for ever.

Portia

Thou may'st, I warrant.[6] We shall have old[7] swearing
That they did give the rings away to men;
But we'll outface[8] them, and outswear them too.
Away, make haste! thou know'st where I will tarry.[9]

Nerissa

Come, good sir, will you show me to this house?   20

[Exeunt

Handwritten annotations:
Shylock will sign now and they'll go straight home.

wants you to come to dinner

takes the ring

They'll say they gave them to men.

Margin notes:

[1] find out where the Jew lives
[2] the deed of gift for Lorenzo and Jessica
[3] It is well that I have caught up with you
[4] on further consideration
[5] wishes to have
[6] I'm sure
[7] a great amount of
[8] stare them down
[9] wait

Summary

The Outwitting Of Husbands

Portia and Nerissa are tying up loose ends before leaving Venice. Portia tells Nerissa to find out where Shylock lives and to get his signature on the deed leaving all his wealth to Lorenzo and Jessica. They intend to reach Belmont before their unsuspecting husbands.

While they are discussing these things, Gratiano catches up with them, bringing from Bassanio the ring Portia wanted and an invitation to dinner. Portia accepts the ring but declines the invitation. She asks Gratiano to take Nerissa to Shylock's house and, before leaving, Nerissa whispers to Portia that she also will trick her husband out of the ring she gave him. Portia likes the idea and anticipates with glee the difficulty both husbands will have in explaining how they gave their wedding rings away.

Scene Analysis

Scene II is a short appendix to the trial scene which develops the ring plot by showing how Bassanio's ring is eventually delivered to Portia and by giving Nerissa the opportunity to get Gratiano's ring also.

The scene continues the happy mood and atmosphere on which the trial scene ended and prepares us for the merry-making of the final Act.

Characters

BASSANIO GIVES IN

The delay in giving the ring to Portia shows the qualms Bassanio has had in parting with something which he vowed never to *'part from, lose or give away'* (Act 3, Sc. II, 172). That he has finally given it exhibits a number of traits in his character – a certain weakness and ineptness combined with a strong sense of gratitude and generosity – and perhaps the ability of a renaissance man to compromise.

Clever Women

Portia and Nerissa have outwitted their husbands and they now propose to *'outface'* and *'outswear'* them further. Like many of the women in Shakespeare's romantic comedies, they are shrewder and more clever than their men.

Act 5

Scene I

*Belmont. The garden in front of Portia's house.
Enter Lorenzo and Jessica*

Lorenzo

The moon shines bright: in such a night as this,
When the sweet wind did gently kiss the trees,
And they did make no noise, in such a night
Troilus[1] methinks mounted the Trojan walls,
And sigh'd his soul toward the Grecian tents,
Where Cressid lay that night.[2]

Jessica

   In such a night
Did Thisbe[3] fearfully o'ertrip[4] the dew,
And saw the lion's shadow ere himself,[5]
And ran dismay'd away.

Lorenzo

   In such a night
Stood Dido[6] with a willow in her hand
Upon the wild sea-banks, and waft[7] her love
To come again to Carthage.

Jessica

   In such a night
Medea[8] gather'd the enchanted herbs
That did renew old Aeson.[9]

Lorenzo

   In such a night
Did Jessica steal[10] from the wealthy Jew,
And with an unthrift love[11] did run from Venice,
As far as Belmont.

Jessica

   In such a night
Did young Lorenzo swear he lov'd her well,
Stealing her soul with many vows of faith,
And ne'er a true one.

Lorenzo

   In such a night   *20*
Did pretty Jessica, like a little shrew,[12]
Slander her love, and he forgave it her.

[handwritten margin note: Lorenzo and Jessica saying how much they love each other]

[1] Troilus was the son of the King of Troy and the faithful lover of Cressida. He is the hero of Shakespeare's play *Troilus and Cressida*

[2] during the Trojan War Cressida was taken away from Troy by the besieging Greeks and deserted Troilus for the Greek Diomede

[3] Thisbe was on her way to a secret rendezvous with her lover Pyramus when she saw a lion and fled, dropping her scarf which the lion mauled. When Pyramus found the scarf he presumed the worst and killed himself. The story appears in comic form at the end of Shakespeare's *A Midsummer Night's Dream*

[4] tiptoe over

[5] before she saw the lion

[6] Dido the Queen of Carthage loved Aeneas the wandering Trojan hero, but he deserted her and sailed to Italy

[7] waved to

[8] Medea was a sorceress who loved Jason and helped him to win the golden fleece

[9] Aeson, Jason's father, was restored to youth by Medea's magic herbs

[10] both 'run away from' and 'rob'

[11] both 'uncalculating love' and 'spendthrift lover'

[12] scolding woman

Jessica

I would out-night you,[13] did nobody come;
But, hark! I hear the footing of a man.

Enter Stephano

Lorenzo

Who comes so fast in silence of the night?

Stephano

A friend.

Lorenzo

A friend! what friend? your name, I pray you, friend.

Stephano

Stephano is my name; and I bring word
My mistress will before the break of day
Be here at Belmont: she doth stray about
By holy crosses,[14] where she kneels and prays
For happy wedlock hours.

Lorenzo

      Who comes with her?

Stephano

None but a holy hermit and her maid.
I pray you, is my master yet return'd?

Lorenzo

He is not, nor we have not heard from him.
But go we in, I pray thee, Jessica,
And ceremoniously let us prepare
Some welcome for the mistress of the house.

Enter Launcelot

Launcelot

Sola, sola![15] wo ha, ho! sola, sola!

Lorenzo

Who calls?

Launcelot

Sola! did you see Master Lorenzo? Master
Lorenzo! sola, sola!

Lorenzo

Leave hollowing, man; here.

Launcelot

Sola! where? where?

Lorenzo

Here.

[13]outdo you at the game of 'in such a night'

[14]roadside shrines

[15]Launcelot is imitating a messenger's horn

Partia is coming 30

Bassanio is coming 40

Launcelot

Tell him there's a post[16] come from my master, with
his horn full of good news: my master will be here ere
morning.   *[Exit*

Lorenzo

Sweet soul, let's in, and there expect their coming.
And yet no matter; why should we go in?   *50*
My friend Stephano, signify,[17] I pray you,
Within the house, your mistress is at hand;
And bring your music forth into the air.

[Exit Stephano

How sweet the moonlight sleeps upon this bank!
Here will we sit, and let the sounds of music
Creep in our ears: soft stillness and the night
Become[18] the touches of sweet harmony.
Sit, Jessica — look how the floor of heaven
Is thick inlaid with patens[19] of bright gold:
There's not the smallest orb[20] which thou behold'st   *60*
But in his motion like an angel sings,
Still quiring[21] to the young-eyed cherubins;[22]
Such harmony is in immortal souls,
But whilst this muddy vesture of decay[23]
Doth grossly close it in,[24] we cannot hear it.

[Enter Musicians

Come, ho! and wake Diana[25] with a hymn:
With sweetest touches pierce your mistress' ear,
And draw her home with music.   *[Music*

Jessica

I am never merry when I hear sweet music.

Lorenzo

The reason is, your spirits are attentive:[26]   *70*
For do but note a wild and wanton[27] herd,
Or race[28] of youthful and unhandled colts,
Fetching[29] mad bounds, bellowing and neighing loud,
Which is the hot condition[30] of their blood;
If they but hear perchance[31] a trumpet sound,
Or any air of music touch their ears,
You shall perceive them make a mutual stand,[32]
Their savage eyes turn'd to a modest[33] gaze
By the sweet power of music: therefore the poet[34]
Did feign[35] that Orpheus[36] drew[37] trees, stones,
        and floods;   *80*
Since naught[38] so stockish,[39] hard, and full of rage,

[16] a messenger boy

[17] announce

[18] suit

[19] small plates
[20] planet, star
[21] making music (the music of the spheres)
[22] angels

[23] this earthly clothing of mortality, i.e. the body
[24] encloses it thickly

[25] goddess of the moon

[26] receptive
[27] playful
[28] breed
[29] making
[30] excited nature
[31] by chance
[32] all stand still together
[33] mild
[34] Ovid
[35] invent the story
[36] a legendary Greek musician who charmed even lifeless objects by the playing of his lyre
[37] attracted
[38] nothing
[39] unmovable

Music is wonderful (handwritten annotation)

But music for the time doth change his nature.
The man that hath no music in himself,
Nor is not mov'd with concord⁴⁰ of sweet sounds,
Is fit for treasons, stratagems,⁴¹ and spoils;⁴²
The motions of his spirit are dull as night,
And his affections dark as Erebus:⁴³
Let no such man be trusted. Mark⁴⁴ the music.

⁴⁰the harmony
⁴¹plots
⁴²acts of plunder

⁴³a dark underworld in Greek mythology
⁴⁴listen to

Enter Portia and Nerissa

Portia

That light we see is burning in my hall.
How far that little candle throws his beams!   90
So shines a good deed in a naughty world.

Glad to be home

Nerissa

When the moon shone, we did not see the candle.

Portia

So doth the greater glory dim the less:
A substitute shines brightly as a king
Until a king be by,⁴⁵ and then his state
Empties itself,⁴⁶ as doth an inland brook
Into the main of waters.⁴⁷ Music! hark!

It's a beautiful night.

⁴⁵be present
⁴⁶his glory is swallowed up
⁴⁷the sea

Nerissa

It is your music, madam, of the house.

Portia

Nothing is good, I see, without respect:⁴⁸
Methinks it sounds much sweeter than by day.   100

⁴⁸without reference to circumstances

Nerissa

Silence bestows that virtue on it, madam.

Portia

The crow doth sing as sweetly as the lark
When neither is attended,⁴⁹ and I think   110
The nightingale, if she should sing by day
When every goose is cackling, would be thought
No better a musician than the wren.
How many things by season season'd are⁵⁰
To their right praise and true perfection!
Peace, ho! the moon sleeps with Endymion,⁵¹
And would not be awak'd!

⁴⁹paid attention to

nighttime makes it special.

⁵⁰are improved by happening at the right time
⁵¹a handsome young shepherd in Greek legend who was so loved by the moon-goddess that she put him to sleep forever

[Music ceases

Lorenzo

    That is the voice,   110
Or I am much deceiv'd, of Portia.

Portia

He knows me, as the blind man knows the cuckoo,   *120*
By the bad voice.

Lorenzo

      Dear lady, welcome home.

Portia

We have been praying for our husbands' welfare,
Which speed,[52] we hope, the better for our words.
Are they return'd?

Are they back.

[52]who prosper

Lorenzo

      Madam, they are not yet;
But there is come a messenger before,
To signify their coming.

Portia

      Go in, Nerissa:
Give order to my servants that they take
No note at all of our being absent hence;   *120*
Nor you, Lorenzo; Jessica, nor you.

Don't say they left.

                     [A trumpet sounds

Lorenzo

Your husband is at hand, I hear his trumpet;
We are no tell-tales, madam, fear you not.

ok.

Portia

This night methinks is but the daylight sick;
It looks a little paler: 'tis a day,
Such as the day is when the sun is hid.

looks cloudy.

    Enter Bassanio, Antonio, Gratiano and their Servants

Bassanio

We should hold day with the Antipodes,[53]
If you would walk in absence of the sun.

[53]have the same daytime as the other side of the world

Portia

Let me give light, but let me not be light;[54]
For a light wife doth make a heavy[55] husband,   *130*
And never be Bassanio so for me:
But God sort all![56] Your are welcome home, my lord.

[54]unfaithful
[55]miserable

[56]decide what will happen

Bassanio

I thank you, madam. Give welcome to my friend:
This is the man, this is Antonio,
To whom I am so infinitely bound.[57]

[57]indebted

Portia

You should in all sense be much bound to him,

For, as I hear, he was much bound for you.

Antonio

No more than I am well acquitted of.[58]

Portia

Sir, you are very welcome to our house:
It must appear in other ways than words,
Therefore I scant[59] this breathing courtesy.[60]

Gratiano

[To Nerissa] By yonder moon I swear you do me
      wrong;
In faith, I gave it to the judge's clerk;
Would he were gelt[61] that had it, for my part,[62]
Since you do take it, love, so much at heart.[63]

Portia

A quarrel, ho, already! what's the matter?

Gratiano

About a hoop of gold, a paltry ring,
That she did give me, whose posy[64] was
For all the world like cutler's poetry[65]
Upon a knife, 'Love me, and leave me not'.

Nerissa

What[66] talk you of the posy, or the value?
You swore to me, when I did give it you,
That you would wear it till your hour of death,
And that it should lie with you in your grave:
Though not for me, yet for your vehement oaths,
You should have been respective[67] and have kept it.
Gave it a judge's clerk! no, God's, my judge,
The clerk will ne'er wear hair on's face that had it.

Gratiano

He will, and if he live to be a man.

Nerissa

Ay, if a woman live to be a man.

Gratiano

Now, by this hand, I gave it to a youth,
A kind of boy, a little scrubbed[68] boy,
No higher than thyself, the judge's clerk.
A prating[69] boy that begg'd it as a fee:
I could not for my heart deny it him.

Portia

You were to blame — I must be plain with you —

Margin glosses:
[58] freed from
[59] cut short
[60] courtesy which consists only of words
[61] castrated
[62] as far as I am concerned
[63] so seriously
[64] an inscription on the inner surface of a ring
[65] like a knife-maker's mottoes
[66] why
[67] mindful of your honour
[68] stunted
[69] talkative

Line numbers: 140, 150, 160

Handwritten annotations: I don't care - it's over; Welcome; Gave it to a man; It's just a ring; trying to get him to admit he gave it a woman; I couldn't say no!

To part so slightly[70] with your wife's first gift;
A thing stuck on with oaths upon your finger,
And so riveted[71] with faith unto your flesh.
I gave my love a ring and made him swear
 Never to part with it: and here he stands;
I dare be sworn for him he would not leave it,
Nor pluck it from his finger, for the wealth
That the world masters.[72] Now, in faith, Gratiano,
You give your wife too unkind a cause of grief:
And 'twere to me,[73] I should be mad at it.

Bassanio

[Aside] Why, I were best to cut my left hand off,
And swear I lost the ring defending it.

Gratiano

My Lord Bassanio gave his ring away
Unto the judge that begg'd it, and indeed
Deserv'd it too; and then the boy, his clerk,
That took some pains in writing, he begg'd mine;
And neither man nor master would take aught
But the two rings.

Portia

       What ring gave you, my lord?
Not that, I hope, which you receiv'd of me.

Bassanio

If I could add a lie unto a fault,
I would deny it; but you see my finger
Hath not the ring upon it — it is gone.

Portia

Even so void[74] is your false heart of truth.
By heaven, I will ne'er come in your bed   190
Until I see the ring.

Nerissa

       Nor I in yours,
Till I again see mine.

Bassanio

       Sweet Portia,
If you did know to whom I gave the ring,
If you did know for whom I gave the ring,
And would conceive for what I gave the ring,
And how unwillingly I left the ring,   When naught would be
accepted but the ring,
You would abate[75] the strength of your displeasure.

[70]easily

[71]welded

[72]possesses

[73]if it happened to me

[74]empty

[75]reduce

[Handwritten margin notes: "Bassanio wouldn't do that! 170"; "He did too! they begged for it 180"; "I can't lie."; "If you knew you wouldn't be mad"]

Portia

[76]power

If you had known the virtue[76] of the ring,
Or half her worthiness that gave the ring,
Or your own honour to contain[77] the ring,
You would not then have parted with the ring.
What man is there so much unreasonable,
If you had pleas'd to have defended it
With any terms of zeal,[78] wanted[79] the modesty
To urge the thing held as a ceremony?[80]
Nerissa teaches me what to believe:
I'll die for 't, but some woman had the ring.

[77]hold on to

[78]enthusiasm
[79]would have lacked
[80]held sacred

Dismisses this 200

Bassanio cheated on her.

Bassanio

No, by my honour, madam, by my soul,
No woman had it, but a civil doctor,[81]
Which did refuse three thousand ducats of me,
And begg'd the ring, the which I did deny him,
And suffer'd[82] him to go displeas'd away;
Even he that had held up the very life
Of my dear friend. What should I say, sweet lady?
I was enforc'd to send it after him.
I was beset[83] with shame and courtesy;
My honour would not let ingratitude
So much besmear[84] it. Pardon me, good lady,
For by these blessed candles of the night,[85]
Had you been there, I think you would have begg'd
The ring of me to give the worthy doctor.

[81]doctor of civil law

[82]allowed

[83]overcome

[84]discredit
[85]i.e. stars

I gave it to a man 210

If you knew you'd be happy I gave it. 220

Portia

Let not that doctor e'er come near my house.
Since he hath got the jewel that I lov'd,
And that which you did swear to keep for me;
I will become as liberal as you ––
I'll not deny him anything I have,
No, not my body, nor my husband's bed.
Know him I shall, I am well sure of it.
Lie not a night from home; watch me like Argus:[86]
If you do not, if I be left alone,
Now by mine honour, which is yet mine own,
I'll have that doctor for my bedfellow.

[86]a monster in classical mythology who has a hundred eyes

If you gave the doctor whatever he wants I will too. 230

Nerissa

[87]be very careful

And I his clerk; therefore be well advis'd[87]
How you do leave me to mine own protection.

Gratiano

[88]catch

Well, do you so: let not me take[88] him, then,

For if I do, I'll mar[89] the young clerk's pen[90].

Antonio

I am th'unhappy subject of these quarrels.

Portia

Sir, grieve not you; you are welcome notwithstanding.

Bassanio

Portia, forgive me this enforced wrong;   240
And in the hearing of these many friends,
I swear to thee, even by thine own fair eyes,
Wherein I see myself—

Portia

      Mark you but that!
In both my eyes he doubly sees himself;
In each eye, one: swear by your double[91] self,
And there's an oath of credit[92].

Bassanio

      Nay, but hear me:
Pardon this fault, and by my soul I swear
I never more will break an oath with thee.

Antonio

I once did lend my body for his wealth[93],
Which, but for him that had your husband's ring,   250
Had quite miscarried: I dare be bound again,
My soul upon the forfeit, that your lord
Will never more break faith advisedly[94].

Portia

Then you shall be his surety[95]. Give him this,
And bid him keep it better than the other.

Antonio

Here, Lord Bassanio; swear to keep this ring.

Bassanio

By heaven! it is the same I gave the doctor!

Portia

I had it of him: pardon me, Bassanio,
For, by the ring, the doctor lay with me.

Nerissa

And pardon me, my gentle Gratiano;   260
For that same scrubbed boy, the doctor's clerk,
In lieu of this[96], last night did lie with me.

Gratiano

Why, this is like the mending of highways

---

[89]ruin
[90]both 'quill' and 'sexual organs'

[91]deceitful
[92]that can be believed

[93]well-being

[94]deliberately

[95]guarantor

[96]in return for

(handwritten margin notes: "I promise he will never do it again"; "I slept with him for it"; "Me too")

⁹⁷roads
⁹⁸husbands whose wives are
   unfaithful to them

⁹⁹coarsely

In summer, where the ways⁹⁷ are fair enough!
What, are we cuckolds⁹⁸ ere we have deserv'd it?

Portia

Speak not so grossly.⁹⁹ You are all amaz'd:
Here is a letter, read it at your leisure,
It comes from Padua, from Bellario:
There you shall find that Portia was the doctor,
Nerissa there her clerk. Lorenzo here
Shall witness I set forth as soon as you,
And even but now return'd; I have not yet
Enter'd my house. Antonio, you are welcome;
And I have better news in store for you
Than you expect: unseal this letter soon;
There you shall find three of your argosies
Are richly come to harbour suddenly.
You shall not know by what strange accident
I chanced on this letter.

Look we were the lawyer and clerk

270

3 ships are ok. He's rich again.

Antonio

    I am dumb.

Bassanio

Were you the doctor, and I knew you not?

280

Gratiano

Were you the clerk that is to make me cuckold?

Nerissa

Ay, but the clerk that never means to do it,
Unless he live until he be a man.

I didn't cheat

Bassanio

Sweet doctor, you shall be my bedfellow:
When I am absent, then lie with my wife.

Antonio

Sweet lady, you have given me life and living;
For here I read for certain that my ships
Are safely come to road.¹⁰⁰

¹⁰⁰to harbour

Portia

    How now, Lorenzo!
My clerk hath some good comforts too for you.

Nerissa

Ay, and I'll give them him without a fee.
There do I give to you and Jessica,
From the rich Jew, a special deed of gift,
After his death, of all he dies possess'd of.

You get Shylock's stuff!

290

Lorenzo

Fair ladies, you drop manna[101] in the way
Of starved people.

101 bread from heaven

Portia

It is almost morning,
And yet I am sure you are not satisfied
Of these events at full. Let us go in;
And charge[102] us there upon inter'gatories[103],
And we will answer all things faithfully.

102 interrogate us
103 with formal questions such
as have to be answered
under oath by a witness
in court

Gratiano

Let it be so: the first inter'gatory
That my Nerissa shall be sworn on is,
Whether till the next night she had rather stay,
Or go to bed now, being two hours to day:
But were the day come, I should wish it dark,
That I were couching[104] with the doctor's clerk.
Well, while I live, I'll fear no other thing
So sore as keeping safe Nerissa's ring.

I'll   *300*

never

mess up

again   104 in bed

[*Exeunt*

Summary

A Happy Ever After

On a still moonlit night in Belmont, Lorenzo and Jessica are strolling in Portia's garden. The night and the romantic atmosphere puts them in mind of the great if sometimes tragic lovers of mythology and antiquity – Troilus and Cressida, Thisbe and Pyramus, Dido and Aeneas, Medea and Jason. It evokes for them also the time and circumstances in which they became lovers and they tease each other lovingly about it all.

Stephano, a servant of Portia's, interrupts them with news that his mistress and Nerissa will return before dawn from the monastery where they have been staying. Launcelot is not far behind with an announcement that Bassanio too will be home before morning. Lorenzo sends Stephano away to announce to the household the imminent return of its lord and lady and to ask Portia's musicians to come outdoors to draw Portia home with music.

When Launcelot and Stephano are gone, Lorenzo and Jessica can indulge a little longer in the night's romantic atmosphere. They sit on a bank and look up at the stars and Lorenzo marvels at the beauty and harmony of the universe. Their happiness is tinged with a slight melancholy, however. Lorenzo regrets that human beings cannot hear the celestial music of the spheres while imprisoned in the body and, when Portia's musicians begin to play, Jessica confesses that sweet music gives her the blues. Lorenzo explains that music heightens sensitivity and he is of the opinion that anyone unmoved by music should not be trusted.

As the lovers listen quietly to the music, Portia and Nerissa arrive home unnoticed. There is a candle lighting in the hall for them and they too stop to listen to the music whose beauty is accentuated by the stillness of the night.

When the music stops, Lorenzo hears Portia's voice and rushes to welcome her home. Portia says that they have been praying for their husbands and emphasises that no one in the household should mention their absence.

A trumpet announces the arrival of Bassanio, Antonio, Gratiano and their servants and Portia graciously welcomes them. But as Bassanio introduces Antonio to his wife, Nerissa is already taking Gratiano to task because of his missing ring. She will not believe for a minute that he gave it to the young clerk of the court: she suspects that another woman is wearing it. Portia also scolds Gratiano for giving away his wife's first present to him. She is confident that Bassanio would never on any account do such a thing and if he did she would be very mad at him indeed. Bassanio is so horrified at what he is hearing that he wonders if it would not be better to cut off his hand and pretend his ring was taken by force. But it is too late for thought: Gratiano has blurted out that Bassanio has in fact given his ring away also. Portia, like Nerissa, succeeds in hiding her amusement and, pretending that she is horrified, she upbraids Bassanio for his false promises. Neither wife will sleep with her husband until the rings are recovered.

Bassanio makes a futile attempt to reason with Portia about what has happened. Portia cannot be convinced, however, that another woman does not have Bassanio's ring. When he insists that the doctor of law has it, she says that she will sleep with the doctor if he ever comes to her house.

Antonio intervenes in an attempt to settle a dispute for which he feels responsible. He pledges on his soul, as he once pledged on his body, that Bassanio will never break his word again. On this security Portia and Nerissa return to their baffled husbands the rings they extracted in Venice. The joke has gone far enough and Portia produces a letter from Bellario explaining the roles she and Nerissa played in the trial scene. Bassanio and Gratiano's bafflement gives way to incredulity and finally admiration.

Portia finally has good news for both Antonio and Lorenzo. Three of Antonio's ships have miraculously arrived home and Lorenzo and Jessica are to inherit all Shylock's wealth when he dies.

Dawn is approaching and Portia suggests that they all retire indoors where they can recount the whole story from start to finish. Gratiano has other things in mind: he would prefer to go to bed with his wife. One thing is certain: he will never give her ring away again.

Scene Analysis

Sending Us Home Happy

If Shakespeare gave all of Act 4 to Venice, he gives all of Act 5 to Belmont. After the turbulence and strain of Venice and the fierce frenzy and passion of the court scene, our senses are calmed and soothed in a wash of moonlight and music, poetry, mirth and romance which obliterates memories of merchant-marring tempests, ducats, bonds, and vicious knives whetted on the sole of the shoe. After the storms, a calm. Shakespeare has bewitched us with the creations of his imagination and held us spellbound for four acts and now he invokes all the magic of his art to weave an enchanting web of happiness and finish the action with *'touches of sweet harmony'*.

How sweet the moonlight sleeps upon this bank!
Here we will sit, and let the sounds of music
Creep in our ears.

(Lorenzo, Act 5, Sc I)

The Sweet Power Of Words And Music

The challenge to the playwright in this scene is that he wished to conjure up an idyllic moonlit night and a garden of Eden for an audience who were looking at a bare stage in broad daylight. The Elizabethan stage had no lighting facilities and performances were given in the afternoon: there were few if any props or special effects. Shakespeare had to say it all with words and his word-pictures and images are so evocative that the moonwashed garden in Belmont has acquired a haunting reality.

Words evoke time and situation. Lorenzo's first words tell the audience that:

> 'The moon shines bright:'

and that it is the kind of night:

> 'When the sweet wind did gently kiss the trees,
> And they did make no noise,'

The word 'night' and the phrase 'in such a night' are repeated so often in the opening dialogue of the young lovers that an audience can be in no doubt about what it should imagine with the mind's eye.

Lorenzo goes on to describe 'The soft stillness and the night' in some of the loveliest poetry in the play:

> 'Sit Jessica — look how the floor of heaven
> Is thick inlaid with patens of bright gold:'

Words evoke memories too, memories of ancient lovers, memories which add to the rich romanticism of the atmosphere.

> 'In such a night
> Stood Dido with a willow in her hand
> Upon the wild sea-banks, and waft her love
> To come again to Carthage.'

If Shakespeare used one special effect, it is 'the sweet power of music' which blends with Lorenzo's words and echoes the unheard singing of angels and the harmony of the planets and welcomes Portia home.

An Earthly Paradise

Belmont's garden is an Arcadian paradise full of the 'concord of sweet sounds'. But it is such a sensually opulent festival of sweetness that there is a danger that it become over-sweet, that the love become sentimental, the music cloying and the poetry mawkish. Perhaps Shakespeare remembers the words he gave to Portia:

> 'O love be moderate; allay thy ecstasy,
> In measure rein thy joy, scant this excess.'

As he takes pains to counterpoint the harmony and sweetness with darker notes which keep our feet upon the ground and remind us that even in a privileged world, troubles are never far away. Clouds occasionally cross the moon and the love stories have echoes of tragedy and unfulfilment: the conversation of the young lovers degenerates into banter and is interrupted by the down-to-earth messages of Stephano and Launcelot: the lovers themselves are sobered with touches of slight melancholy – Lorenzo bemoans the limitations of *'this muddy vesture of decay'* and Jessica is *'never merry'* when she hears *'sweet music'*. There is also a reminder of the man for whom music was so much *'vile squealing'* and who was *'fit for treasons, stratagems, and spoils'*. For all its radiance, the happiness shines like Portia's candle — somewhat like *'a good deed in a naughty world'*.

The Ring Plot: A Comic End

What threatens the harmony most explicitly, however, is a double quarrel, *'About a hoop of gold, a paltry ring'*

which two wives appear to take *'so much at heart'*. The pure comedy of two husbands being rounded upon by their wives for an *'enforced wrong'* makes plain Shakespeare's intent that the play end on a comic note.

As with much of the humour in the play, its peculiar quality lies in the dramatic irony which occurs when the audience knows something of which some of the characters are unaware. When Gratiano tells Nerissa that he gave his ring to:

> *'... a little scrubbed boy,*
> *No higher than thyself,'*

he is unaware of the comic aptness of his description or of how she might be insulted by his words. Nor does he know how true Nerissa's words are when she tells him:

> *'The clerk will ne'er wear hair on's face that had it.'*

Happy Ever After

It is an unreal quarrel, however; merely an echo of the trouble that is past. When it passes, the sense of relief and euphoria is nevertheless greater than ever. Love, generosity and good humour have triumphed and with the salvation of Antonio's fortunes the last cloud disappears.

Characters

A LAST LOOK AT PORTIA

Portia is missing for the first part of this scene for compelling reasons: she has to change her clothes and travel from Venice to Belmont in less than one hundred lines!

As Portia catches her breath on arrival in Belmont, the first thing she notices is the candle lighting in her hall:

> *'So shines a good deed in a naughty world.'*

She is perhaps thinking of how Bassanio left such a blissful scene to help a friend in need or she may be taking deserved satisfaction in her own role in saving Antonio.

Portia's musicians *'draw her home with music'* and as the sweetness of the sound is intensified by the stillness of the night, Portia notes that there is a time and place for everything:

> *'How many things by season season'd are*
> *To their right praise and true perfection!'*

It is in many ways a fitting comment on the roles she has acted in the play. When the season called for it she has been a witty young heiress, a widely sought object of desire, a gracious hostess, a mischievous tomboy, a loving wife and a learned doctor of law. She has played each role with resourcefulness and relish and an irrepressible spirit of playfulness which will be our abiding memory of her.

She now resumes the role of gracious hostess as she welcomes Antonio to Belmont.

> *'Sir, you are very welcome to our house:*
> *It must appear in other ways than words,*
> *Therefore I scant this breathing courtesy.'*

The real reason why Portia is cutting short her verbal politeness is that she has one last role to play. It is the role of a jealous and angry wife and she plays it with enthusiasm and perversity. She enjoys especially the comic irony of her own words:

> *'I'll die for 't, but some woman had the ring.'*

Behind the acted role, however, Portia remains a lady to the end. If she knows the seasonality of things she also has a sense of proportion which does not carry a joke too far. She does not wish to embarrass Antonio further and Bassanio has suffered enough. The *'sweet lady'* ends the scene dispensing *'life and living'* and *'good comforts'* to all around her.

BASSANIO'S LAST TRIAL

Bassanio returns to Belmont with princely bearing and to the sound of trumpets. In going to Venice to save his friend he has done *'a good deed in a naughty world'*.

But he has also broken his promise to Portia and he is about to be taken down a peg:

> *'Even so void is your false heart of truth.'*

Bassanio cannot bear the prospect of falling in Portia's esteem:

> *'Why, I were best to cut my left hand off,*
> *And swear I lost the ring defending it.'*

He also knows that there is some truth in Portia's remarks. For whatever good reasons and however unwillingly, he has not:

'defended...
With any terms of zeal...
... the thing held as a ceremony?'

He has been too 'liberal' with Portia's ring as he has been liberal with Antonio's and Portia's money heretofore. The serious note in Portia's jibes is that carefree liberality can amount to infidelity:

'I will become as liberal as you —
I'll not deny him anything I have,'

Behind the humour the character of Bassanio is on trial. He acquits himself admirably, however; he will not 'add a lie unto a fault' and puts none of the blame on Antonio. If his 'honour to contain the ring' has been impeached, he defends his 'honour' vehemently:

'My honour' he says,
'would not let ingratitude
...besmear it.'

Portia was correct when she surmised that Bassanio would not part with her ring:

'for the wealth
That the world masters.'

But gratitude and generosity of heart are more compelling than wealth for Bassanio and when he was 'beset with shame and courtesy' he gave the ring away.

The man who started the play as an improvident fortune hunter has erred in the end only through his generosity.

ANTONIO

Generous And Enigmatic To The End

Antonio has been the most generous character in the play, and though he has been chastened by experience, he remains generous to the end.

'...I dare be bound again,
My soul upon the forfeit,'

The play's happy ending would be incomplete if Antonio went unrewarded for his courage and goodness.

'Sweet lady, you have given me life and living;
For here I read for certain that my ships
Are safely come to road.'

Antonio remains, nevertheless, an essentially lonely and enigmatic figure. He has always been on the periphery of the action even if he has been 'th' unhappy subject of these quarrels.'

He has had a surprisingly small role considering that the play was named after him and though he is part of the play's happy ending, there is an extent to which he remains the odd man out in the midst of all the happy lovers.

GRATIANO

The Last Word

Gratiano enters the action of the last scene on a note of injured innocence:

> *'By yonder moon I swear you do me wrong;'*

He is an insensitive man who does not understand why a *'paltry ring'* should be taken *'so much at heart'* and he confirms his reputation as a 'big mouth' by spilling the beans on Bassanio.

> *'My Lord Bassanio gave his ring away*
> *Unto the judge that begg'd it,'*

His humour is so vulgar and bawdy that Portia asks him to *'Speak not so grossly,'*

We are not surprised that he has the last word in the play:

> *'Well, while I live, I'll fear no other thing*
> *So sore as keeping safe Nerissa's ring.'*

NERISSA

A Little Scrubbed Boy!

Nerissa has picked up much of Portia's wit and philosophy and she will need it all if she is to tame Gratiano's *'skipping spirit'*. She takes him to task with such relish, however, that she leaves us in no doubt that she will be well able for him:

> *'You swore to me, when I did give it you,*
> *That you would wear it till your hour of death,'*

They are well matched. If *'Gratiano speaks an infinite deal of nothing,'* Nerissa is equally capable of *'prating'*. And if the inscription on the ring is anything to go by, Nerissa can be as banal as her husband.

> *'Love me, and leave me not.'*

Her wit, however, has an irony of which he would be incapable.

> *'The clerk will ne'er wear hair on's face that had it.'*

It promises to be a fiery relationship.

JESSICA

Peace At Last

Jessica's loving nature has blossomed in the security and tranquility of her new home in Belmont. She receives from Lorenzo the love and affection of which she was starved in her father's house and this, more than the financial legacy of his enforced will, represents:

> '...manna in the way
> Of starved people.'

Reminders persist, however, of the dubious circumstances in which her happiness began and of the austere *'hell'* in which she grew up:

> '... In such a night
> Did Jessica steal from the wealthy Jew,
> And with an unthrift love did run from Venice,
> As far as Belmont.'

That Jessica is *'never merry'* when she hears *'sweet music'* may be a legacy also – an unhappy one, from the *'sober house'* whose windows were barred to the *'sound of shallow foppery.'*

LORENZO

Poetic Knight-Errant

Portia has held Lorenzo in sufficient esteem to leave him in charge of her household during her absence. Lorenzo is made from the same mould as Bassanio and is a fitting substitute for his lord.

> 'A substitute shines brightly as a king
> Until a king be by,'

For a minor character, Lorenzo is given some of the play's most beautiful lines. His poetry ranges over the beauty of the night:

> 'How sweet the moonlight sleeps upon this bank!'

the motion of the stars:

> 'There's not the smallest orb which thou behold'st
> But in his motion like an angel sings;' and the

> 'sweet power of music'

> 'The man that hath no music in himself,
> Nor is not mov'd with concord of sweet sounds,
> Is fit for treasons, stratagems, and spoils;'

Lorenzo is above all the knight-errant who loved Jessica back to wholeness and who is rewarded in the 'happy ever-after' with riches which *'drop'* on him like *'manna'* from heaven.

Part 3

FURTHER STUDY

The Categories of Shakespeare's Plays

Shakespeare's plays are traditionally divided into three categories: comedies, histories and tragedies. These categories are not always helpful as the so-called tragedies have elements of history and comedy, the comedies have elements of tragedy, and so on. Furthermore, there are 'problem plays' which do not fit easily into any one category. To clarify this situation, further categories are sometimes added. Comedies, for instance, are described as romantic comedies, tragi-comedies or dark comedies.

The Merchant of Venice is traditionally regarded as one of Shakespeare's comedies and is further categorised as a romantic comedy. It is sometimes described as a tragi-comedy.

Romantic Comedy

Romance

The term 'romantic' gives most difficulty to the modern student when applied to *The Merchant of Venice*. A 'romance' in modern parlance is taken to mean a love affair and 'romantic' is used to describe an atmosphere or feeling. In modern literature 'romance' stands for lightweight commercial fiction produced for wish-fulfilment and day-dreaming. The modern student tends to see 'romance' and 'romantic', therefore, as referring to the relationship of Bassanio and Portia or Jessica and Lorenzo, but if his or her understanding stops here, he or she will have missed much of the point.

To understand the meaning of the word 'romance', one has to know something of its history. The word has its remote sources in Greek literature, and in medieval times it had come to refer to stories of courtly love and adventure which were full of the qualities associated with the new vernacular languages derived from Latin (i.e. the 'romance languages', e.g. French). These stories were full of chivalry and knight-errantry, lofty sentiments and high ideals. *Don Quixote* by Cervantes is a celebrated example and parody of the genre.

To the romance writer, the highest ideal of all and the most important of human experiences was love. And love always entailed chivalry. Romance stories were stories of extravagant and far-fetched adventure, success stories whose happy endings depended on luck and surviving an ordeal and whose conventions included coincidence, mistaken identity and poetic justice. These stories promoted an enjoyment of the marvellous and the wonderful, and transported readers beyond the limits of ordinary life. Like their modern counterparts, they ministered to day-dreams and vagrancy of the imagination.

The casket story in *The Merchant of Venice* is a good example of the romantic in its fullest sense. The play as a whole is rich in extravagant adventure, knight-errantry and courtly love.

It has its disguises, its ordeals and its happy endings. Venice and Belmont are essentially romantic places and Shylock, Antonio, Bassanio and Portia are, each in their own way, romantic figures.

Comedy

But *The Merchant of Venice* is not merely a romance, it is a romantic comedy. The comic is that quality in action or situation, character or manners which amuses or provokes laughter. We laugh because there is something incongruous in what we see or hear, something which deviates from or contrasts with what is normally expected.

Comedy is drama whose object is to amuse. It is a light-hearted and detached comment on the world. At one extreme it is a farce, where the mind takes a complete holiday; at the other extreme, it can be toned with irony and satire. In the middle ages comedy meant simply a story with a happy ending.

The elements of comedy are easily identified in *The Merchant of Venice*. The episode of the rings, for example, is pure comedy of situation. We can also identify elements of comedy in Portia's comments on the foibles of her suitors, Launcelot's overblown vocabulary, Gobbo's simplicity, Shylock's miserliness, the folly of Morocco and Arragon, and so on.

An Uneasy Comedy

But if *The Merchant of Venice* is a comedy, it is an uneasy one. Comedy and romance cannot account for all the elements in the play. As early as 1709, Nicholas Rowe thought that Shylock's contribution to the play made it a tragedy: 'Though we have seen that play receiv'd and acted as a comedy, and the part of the Jew perform'd by an excellent comedian, yet I cannot but think it was design'd tragically by the author. There appears in it such a deadly spirit of revenge, such a savage fierceness and fellness, and such a bloody designation of cruelty and mischief, as cannot agree either with the style or characters of comedy.'

The problem, as another early critic (Heine) saw it, was that although 'Shakespeare intended to write a comedy… he was too great a man to succeed'. Shakespeare, the argument goes, put so much imaginative effort into making his Jew a credible human being that we cannot laugh at him whole-heartedly. Shylock's humanity, it is argued, goes beyond what would be appropriate to the villain of mere comedy.

Shakespeare's Intention

Shylock's humanity is indeed very real and his predicament is imaginatively grasped, but this does not mean that *The Merchant of Venice* is a tragedy: the title of the play is not *The Jew of Venice* and Act 5 displays the final intention and tone of the play.

It can be said, however, that Shylock has inserted an element of tragedy into the framework of romantic comedy and that the temper of the play is tragic as long as he holds the stage. The more you take Shylock to be the central figure of the play, the more tragic the play becomes. It can also be said that the intensity of Shylock's hatred and the physical reality of his threat to Antonio takes away that immunity and detachment from suffering on which comedy depends. Because of this, critics have sometimes found it helpful to refer to *The Merchant of Venice* as a tragi-comedy, a story of tragedy averted. Tragi-comedy does not conflict with romance or comedy, however; as we have seen, one of the conventions of romance was an ordeal survived, and comedy always had a happy ending.

Asking what genre *The Merchant of Venice* falls into is akin to asking which of its parents or ancestors a child looks like or takes after. Some see the traits of one family, some see the traits of another. The child probably has traits of all sides and will reflect one side or the other more or less according to time and circumstances. Ultimately, the child is his or her own self.

The Merchant of Venice reflects many of the disparate elements of drama and in different times down through its history, the romantic, or the comic, or the tragic have been emphasised, all validly, reflecting the moods, insights and needs of different generations of producers, actors and theatre-goers.

Perhaps it is partly the secret of the play's continual freshness that it cannot be categorised easily or murdered by analysis, that it insists on reflecting the ambivalence of which life is made. It continues to engage and exercise the intellect as well as the imagination.

Themes in the Play

It has been said that *The Merchant of Venice* is a theme-hunter's delight. Many of the themes below have been touched upon in the scene analyses: they are listed here so that they may be further pursued as threads for thought, subjects for discussion, topics for essays or headings for general project work on the play.

Theme 1   **Right and Wrong Judgement**
the danger of mistaking appearance for reality
the fragility of judgements made by the eye
the fatal fascination of reason
deception and disguise
spiritual stupidity
wit

Theme 2   **Justice**
the inhumanity of mere justice
the triumph of mercy over justice
poetic justice
the letter and spirit of the law
Old Law and New

Theme 3   **Love**
ideal love
sexual love
friendship
the nobility of friendship
the true essence of friendship
loyalty
obligation
sacrifice
love's triumph over adversity
the permanence of things of the heart

Theme 4   **Generosity and its Rewards**

Theme 5	**Wealth**	

Theme 5   **Wealth**
wealth, worldly and otherworldly
the quest for fortune
the instability and transience of worldly wealth
usury
money
avarice
love's wealth

Theme 6   **Beauty**
the quest for beauty
the transience of sensory beauty
the beauty of the night

Theme 7   **Hatred**
revenge and its cruelty
revenge – legal and illegal

Theme 8   **Racial Persecution**
Jewry
the humanity of outcasts

Theme 9   **Chance**

Theme 10   **Harmony**
order
music
the music of the spheres
disorder

Theme 11   **Hell**

Theme 12   **Loneliness**

Theme 13   **Metals**

Theme 14   **The Strength and Wisdom of Man**

Theme 15   **The Intellect and Wit of Woman**

Context Questions on the Play

Understanding the context of certain extracts from *The Merchant of Venice* will give students a better knowledge of the play as a whole.

Briefly explain the following extracts, giving the name of the speaker and the context of the extract:

1. *'The devil can cite Scripture for his purpose.*
   An evil soul, producing holy witness,
   Is like a villain with a smiling cheek.'

2. *'How far that little candle throws his beams!*
   So shines a good deed in a naughty world.'

3. *'It is a good divine that follows his own instructions.'*

4. *'So may the outward shows be least themselves*
   The world is still deceiv'd with ornament.'

5. *'Wrest once the law to your authority:*
   To do a great thing, do a little wrong.'

6. *'If I can catch him once upon the hip,*
   I will feed fat the ancient grudge I bear him.'

7. *'There are a sort of men whose visages*
   Do cream and mantle like a standing pond,
   And do a wilful stillness entertain,
   With purpose to be dress'd in an opinion
   Of wisdom, gravity, profound conceit.'

8. *'How many things by season season'd are*
   To their right praise and true perfection!'

9. *'Be assured*
   My purse, my person, my extremest means
   Lie all unlock'd to your occasions.'

10. *'The crow doth sing as sweetly as the lark*
    When neither is attended.'

Answering Questions on Context

In the case of each of the extracts, simply do the following:

(a) Name the speaker.

(b) Name the person or persons to whom he or she is speaking. If the lines are from a soliloquy, simply say so.

(c) Give your understanding of the lines.

(d) Explain what is happening in the play at the time when the lines are spoken.

Example

> *'How far that little candle throws his beams!*
> *So shines a good deed in a naughty world.'*

Inter Cert. 1973

Sample Answer

(a) Portia

(b) Nerissa

(c) As she returns to Belmont at night, Portia notices that there is a candle burning in her hall which throws its light out into the surrounding darkness. Portia compares the radiance of the candle to the effect of a good act and the example it gives to a bad world.

(d) These lines are spoken as Portia and Nerissa arrive home unnoticed after their disguised expedition to Venice where Portia saved Antonio in the trial scene. Portia may be patting herself on the back for her efforts to save Antonio or she may be thinking of the way Bassanio abandoned his new-found bliss to return to Venice to help a friend in need.

Further Context Questions

1. *'Thou call'dst me dog before thou hadst a cause,*
   But since I am a dog, beware my fangs.'

2. *'All things that are,*
   Are with more spirit chased than enjoy'd.'

3. *'You have too much respect upon the world;*
   They lose it that do buy it with much care.'

4. *'I am th' unhappy subject of these quarrels.'*

5. *'They are as sick that surfeit with too much as they that starve with nothing.'*

6. '*I was beset with shame and courtesy;*
    My honour would not let ingratitude
    So much besmear it.'

7. '*A golden mind stoops not to shows of dross.*'

8. '*There is no vice so simple but assumes*
    Some mark of virtue on his outward parts.'

9. '*There is not one among them but I dote on his very absence.*'

10. '*I am never merry when I hear sweet music.*'

11. '*Hates any man the thing he would not kill?*'

12. '*The brain may devise laws for the blood,*
    But a hot temper leaps o'er a cold decree.'

13. '*I like not fair terms and a villain's mind.*'

14. '*A halter gratis; nothing else, for God's sake!*'

15. '*I have within my mind*
    A thousand raw tricks of these bragging jacks,
    Which I will practise.'

16. '*The villiany you teach me I will execute,*
    And it shall go hard but I will better the instruction.'

17. '*O these deliberate fools! when they do choose,*
    They have the wisdom by their wit to lose.'

18. '*But love is blind, and lovers cannot see*
    The pretty follies that themselves commit.'

19. '*It is a wise father that knows his own child.*'

20. '*My ventures are not in one bottom trusted,*
    Nor to one place; nor is my whole estate
    Upon the fortune of this present year.'

21. '*Thou art too wild, too rude, and bold of voice.*'

22. '*Let not the sound of shallow foppery enter*
    My sober house.'

23. '*O these naughty times*
    Put bars between the owners and their rights.'

24. '*I am a tainted wether of the flock,*
    Meetest for death.'

25. '*Our house is hell, and thou, a merry devil,*
    Didst rob it of some taste of tediousness.'

26. '*He is well paid that is well satisfied.*'

27. 'A substitute shines brightly as a king
    Until a king be by, and then his state
    Empties itself, as doth an inland brook
    Into the main of waters.'

28. 'Alack, what heinous sin is it in me
    To be asham'd to be my father's child!'

29. 'O ten times faster Venus' pigeons fly
    To seal love's bonds new-made, than they are wont
    To keep obliged faith unforfeited!'

30. 'Wilt thou show the whole wealth of thy wit in an instant?'

31. 'The man that hath no music in himself,
    Nor is not mov'd with concord of sweet sounds,
    Is fit for treasons, stratagems, and spoils.'

32. 'Fast bind, fast find';
    A proverb never stale in thrifty mind.'

33. 'I think he only loves the world for him.'

34. 'If you do love me, you will find me out.'

35. 'What man is there so much unreasonable,
    If you had pleas'd to have defended it
    With any terms of zeal, wanted the modesty
    To urge the thing held as a ceremony?'

Questions on Individual Scenes

N.B. Give reasons for all answers and support them wherever possible with relevant quotations or references.

Act 1

Scene I

1. Describe the atmosphere of the first scene of the play.

2. Salerio and Gratiano have differing views as to why Antonio is depressed.
   (a) What are their views respectively?
   (b) Why do you think Antonio is sad?

3. What impression does Bassanio make on you in the opening scene?

4. For what purpose does Bassanio require a loan?

5. How is Portia described in this scene?

Scene II

1. Portia, like Antonio, is suffering from melancholy. Can you suggest a reason as to why this is so?

2. What conditions has her father's will imposed on Portia?

3. What are the national characteristics which Portia attributes to the six suitors who have come to woo her thus far?

4. What impression has Bassanio made on Portia?

5. Nerissa is quite a philosopher. What do you think?

Scene III

1. What are our first impressions of Shylock?

2. (a) What is usury?
   (b) Why does Antonio object to usury?
   (c) How does Shylock defend it?

3. (a) Why does Shylock hate Antonio?
   (b) To what extent is he justified?

4. Does Shylock really wish to let bygones be bygones or does he intend to kill Antonio?

5. What are the terms of the bond under which Shylock lends money to Antonio?

6. Antonio and Bassanio both display great naivety in this scene. Explain.

7. Compare and contrast Venice and Belmont as portrayed in the first act of the play.

Act 2

Scene I

1. (a) How does Morocco describe himself?
   (b) Why is he so defensive and apprehensive?

2. Portia's *'destiny'* has been reduced to a *'lottery'*. Explain.

3. What conditions follow a wrong choice at the caskets?

Scene II

1. Define the term 'malapropism' and give examples of it from the speech of Launcelot.

2. For what reasons does Launcelot decide to leave Shylock's service?

3. Why is Bassanio reluctant to take Gratiano with him to Belmont?

4. How does this scene develop the overall plot of the play?

Scene III

1. Describe the parting scene between Launcelot and Jessica.

2. What impressions of Shylock's house are given in this scene?

3. Describe the atmosphere of the scene.

Scene IV

1. (a) What is a masque?
   (b) Why were Lorenzo and his friends preparing a masque?
   (c) Why did the masque never happen?

2. What was the substance of the letter which Jessica sent to Lorenzo?

3. What do we learn of Jessica's character in this scene?

Scene V

1. Why is Shylock pleased that Launcelot is going to work for Bassanio?

2. Is there any evidence in this scene that Shylock had any affection for his former servant?

3. (a) Define the term 'dramatic irony'.
   (b) Give an example of dramatic irony from this scene.

4. What does this scene tell us about Shylock's attitude to merry-making, fun, music and life in general?

Scene VI

1. What do we learn from this scene of (a) the theatre, (b) the actors of Shakespeare's day?

2. 'Jessica has inherited some of her father's avarice and does not deserve the praise that Lorenzo gives her.' What to you think?

3. What news does Antonio bring at the end of the scene?

Scene VII

1. What do we learn of the device of the caskets in this scene?

2. What are the inscriptions which the respective caskets bear?

3. Why does Morocco reject the silver and lead caskets in favour of the gold one?

4. Should the Prince of Morocco be played only for laughs or is he worthy of more consideration?

5. What great theme of Shakespeare's is illustrated in this scene?

Scene VIII

1. (a) How has Shylock taken the elopement of his daughter and the loss of his jewels?
   (b) Why has Shakespeare not represented Shylock's initial reaction upon the stage?

2. What ominous indications are there for Antonio's coming fate in this scene?

3. What does it mean to say that Salerio and Solanio act as a 'chorus'?

4. What do we learn here of the relationship of Antonio and Bassanio?

Scene IX

1. (a) What trait in Arragon's character contributes most to his downfall?
   (b) What line of argument does he use to decide upon the silver casket?

2. What three conditions were imposed on each of Portia's suitors?

3. What does this scene tell us of the frame of mind Bassanio must be in if he is to choose the right casket?

4. Why do you think there have been so many scenes in Act 2?

Act 3

Scene I

1. 'What is often seen as Shylock's plea for tolerance is in reality his justification of his inhuman intentions.' What do you think?

2. What evidence is there in this scene that Shylock has genuine human feelings under his harsh exterior?

3. Write a note on the humour in this scene.

4. What is Tubal's function in the play?

5. Why is this scene written in prose?

Scene II

1. Why is this such an important scene?

2. How does Portia show her love for Bassanio before he makes his choice at the caskets?

3. What role does music play in this scene?

4. By what examples does Bassanio establish that the world is so often deceived by external appearances?

5. Why is it so significant that Jessica has heard her father voice his intention to have flesh rather than money from Antonio?

6. (a) Who was Midas?

   (b) Does he have any connection with Shylock?

7. How does Bassanio describe Antonio?

8. What are the three kinds of love which are illustrated in this scene? Give examples of each.

Scene III

1. This scene illuminates Shylock's purpose and motives. Explain.

2. What evidence is there in this scene that Antonio has changed his attitude towards his old adversary?

3. Compare and contrast Antonio's generosity with Shylock's greed and spitefulness.

4. Why is the Duke unable to interfere in the dispute between Antonio and Shylock?

Scene IV

1. Compare Portia's resourcefulness in this scene with Antonio's passive fatalism as exhibited in the previous scene.

2. What, according to Portia, is the true essence of friendship?

3. What does this scene tell us of the mannerisms of young men in Shakespeare's day?

Scene V

1. What are the dramatic purposes of this scene?

2. Has Jessica changed in any way since her arrival in Belmont?

3. What does Jessica think of Portia?

4. How appropriate is the term 'wit-snapper' as applied to Launcelot?

5. What attitudes to pregnancy, illegitimacy and women are illustrated in this scene?

Act 4

Scene I

1. Describe the manner in which Antonio bears up to the difficult circumstances of the trial scene.

2. What does the Duke have to say to Shylock at the beginning of the hearing?

3. Give an outline of the arguments put forward by Shylock to support his case.

4. Summarise, in your own words, what Portia says about mercy.

5. (a) Outline the stages in the destruction of Shylock.
   (b) To what extent is it true to say that Portia gave Shylock every opportunity to save his soul?

6. Shylock's view of the law is not only defeated; it is sent up in a grim parody. What do you think?

7. Would Shylock really have killed Antonio?

8. Did Shylock get his 'just desserts' or was the punishment disproportionate to the crime? Do the Christians afford him the mercy of which they preach?

9. How should Shylock's exit be played?

10. Describe Gratiano's conduct throughout the trial scene.

11. Should the play end here?

12. Write a note on the humour of the trial scene.

Scene II

1. (a) What is the purpose of the ring plot?
   (b) Where does it begin?
   (c) What contribution does this scene make to the ring plot?

2. Why did Shakespeare not allow Portia to receive the ring at the end of the previous scene?

3. What evidence is there in this scene to suggest the view that women are smarter than men?

Act 5

Scene I

1. (a) Describe the atmosphere of the play's final scene.
   (b) How is this atmosphere achieved?

2. Write a note on the poetry of Lorenzo.

3. What is the purpose of this scene?

4. Do you consider this scene to be a fitting end to the play?

5. 'Although much of this scene is heavenly there are traces and echoes of the not-so-heavenly.' Explain.

6. (a) What excuses does Bassanio put forward to justify his giving the ring away?
   (b) To what extent does he redeem himself?

7. 'Gratiano and Nerissa are well matched!' What do you think?

8. What is our final impression of Portia?

9. 'There is an extent to which Antonio remains the odd man out.' What do you think?

Examination Questions

JUNIOR CERTIFICATE ENGLISH: ORDINARY LEVEL

2004

Section 6: Drama, Question E

Name a **PLAY** or **FILM** you have studied in which a disagreement occurs.

Using **ONE** of the following headings, write about the play or film.

- The scene I liked best.
- The character I found most interesting.
- Why I found the play/film enjoyable.
- Why I did not enjoy the play/film.   (20)

2005

Section 6: Drama, Question E

Name a **PLAY** or **FILM** you have studied.

Pick the scene you remember best from the play or the film and write about:

- what exactly happened
- how any **ONE** character behaved
- what especially makes you remember the scene you have chosen.   (20)

2006

Section 6: Drama, Question E

Name a **PLAY** or **FILM** you have studied in which a disagreement occurs.

  (a) What caused the disagreement?

  (b) Was the disagreement settled? Why? Why not?

  (c) Were you satisfied with the ending? Give reasons for your answer.   (20)

2007

Section 6: Drama, Question E

  1. Name a play or film you have studied in which something very unexpected
     happens. Describe the unexpected event and explain why it was unexpected.   (10)

  2. Did the unexpected event add to your enjoyment of the studied play or film?
     Explain why/why not?   (10)

2008

Section 6: Drama, Question E

Name a **PLAY** or **FILM** you have studied in which a character has an important dream or
ambition which he/she succeeds or fails in making real.

  • What was the dream or ambition?

  • How did it succeed or fail?

  • What effect did this success or failure have on the character in question?

  • Would you recommend this film or play to your friends? Why/Why not?

                                                                                  (20)

JUNIOR CERTIFICATE ENGLISH: HIGHER LEVEL

2004

Section 1: Drama

Question Two: Answer **EITHER 1 OR 2**.

  1. Name a play you have studied in which one character rebels against another. With
     which character did you have more sympathy? Give reasons for your answer making
     reference to the play.   (30)

OR

  2. Name a play you have studied.
     Choose a scene from this play you found either happy **or** sad.
     Describe how the playwright conveys this happiness **or** sadness.   (30)

2005

Section 1: Drama

Question Two: Answer **EITHER 1 OR 2**.

1. Select a play you have studied and choose from it a scene where conflict occurs.
   (a) Outline what happens in this scene.　　　　　　　　　　　　　　　　(10)
   (b) What are the underlying causes of the conflict in this scene?
   Support your answer by reference to the play as a whole.　　　　　　　　(20)

OR

2. Choose your favourite character from a play you have studied.
   (a) Why do you find this character interesting? Support your answer by reference to the text.　　　　　　　　　　　　　　　　　　　　　　　　　　　(10)
   (b) Discuss the relationship between your chosen character and **ONE** other character in the play. Refer to the text in support of your answer.　　　　　　(20)

2006

Question Two: Answer **EITHER 1 OR 2**.

1. Consider a character from a play you have studied. Choose a significant time of *either* good luck *or* bad luck which this character experiences.
   (a) Briefly describe this experience of good luck *or* bad luck.　　　　　(15)
   (b) Discuss how the character deals with it in the play.　　　　　　　　(15)

OR

2. 'Plays teach us lessons about life.'
   Choose any play you have studied and explain how it has made you aware of any one of the following:

   Love or Death or Conflict or Harmony.

   Explain your answer by reference to your chosen play.　　　　　　　　(30)

2007

Section 1: Drama

Question Two: Answer **EITHER 1 OR 2**.

1. Name a play you have studied and state what you think is its main idea and/or message. Explain how this main idea and/or message is communicated in the play.　(30)

OR

2. You have been asked to recommend a play for students studying for the Junior Certificate. Would you recommend the play you have studied for this examination? Give reasons based on close reference to your chosen text.   (30)

2008

Section 1: Drama

Question Two: Answer **EITHER 1 OR 2.**

1. Many dramas feature characters that are either winners or losers. Choose a character from a play that you have studied who falls into one of these categories.
   (a) Describe how your chosen character is either a winner or a loser.   (10)
   (b) Choose another character who has a relationship with your chosen character, and explain the importance of this relationship.
       Support your answer with references to your studied text.   (20)

OR

2. Imagine you are preparing a programme for a class production of a play you have studied. The production team, of which you are a part, has asked you to contribute to the programme.
   (a) Write character profiles for two characters who have a significant role in the play.   (15)
   (b) Write an introduction to the play focusing especially on its theme(s).   (15)

To keep the programme to an appropriate length you will need to write approximately 200 words for task (a) and approximately 200 words for task (b).

General Questions on the Play

1. Show how Shakespeare has skilfully interwoven the different stories and sub-plots of which the play is made.

2. 'The Merchant of Venice is a play about two worlds – the harsh mercantile world of Venice and the romantic and decadent world of Belmont.' Discuss this statement supporting your answer with relevant quotation or reference.

3. 'Although the play takes its title from Antonio, Shylock is really the central character of the play.' Discuss.

4. 'Act 1 Scene III bristles with animosity.' Discuss this statement, supporting your answer with relevant quotation and reference from the scene.

5. 'Shylock is an upright and moral figure who is twisted and thwarted by a society which has no moral core.' Would you agree with this view? Quote in support of your opinions.

6. Portia has been described as Shakespeare's first lady of the Renaissance. What features of Portia's character do you find attactive or unattractive? Support your answer by quotation or reference.

7. Compare and contrast the attitudes to wealth shown in the play by any two of the following characters: Antonio; Bassanio; Shylock; Portia.

8. 'Shakespeare's topics are timeless and his themes eternal.' Discuss this statement, indicating what you consider to be the central theme of the play.

9. 'The character of Shylock is in conflict with the comic intention of the play.' Discuss.

10. 'Bassanio is full of fine sentiments but he produces no significant moral action.' Is this a fair description of his character? Discuss the view that Bassanio is unworthy of Portia or Antonio.

11. 'Antonio is the most unremarkable character ever to have had a play named after him.' Would you agree with this view? Quote in support of your opinions.

12. 'The lottery of the caskets was devised by Portia's father as a test of character.' Comment on this statement and point out the differences in character of the three suitors as shown by their respective choices.

13. 'The final Act is really superfluous to the drama.' Discuss the view that the play should end with Act 4.

14. The Merchant of Venice has elements both of tragedy and comedy, but it cannot be described satisfactorily as either one or the other.' Discuss.

15. 'Shylock remains part of the vision of the play long after he is gone.' Discuss.

16. Discuss the contribution made to the play by any two of the following characters:
    (1) Gratiano; (2) Lorenzo; (3) Jessica; (4) Nerissa; (5) Launcelot.

17. It has been said that The Merchant of Venice has no real hero or heroine. Would you agree with that opinion? Who, in your opinion, has the best claim to the title of hero or heroine?

18. 'The Merchant of Venice is an anti-Semitic play and should no longer be performed.' What is your opinion of this statement? Give reasons for your answer.

19. Do you consider The Merchant of Venice to be a relevant or an irrelevant play? Give reasons for your answer.

20. 'The Merchant of Venice continues to be performed and to attract large audiences.' Can you account for its continuing popularity?